MILS MULIAINA

LIVING THE DREAM MILS MULIAINA

with Lynn McConnell

Hodder Moa

National Library of New Zealand Cataloguing-in-Publication Data
McConnell, Lynn.
Mils Muliaina : living the dream / Lynn McConnell.
ISBN 978-1-86971-166-5
1. Muliaina, Mils. 2. Rugby Union football players—New Zealand—Biography.
I. Title.
796.333092—dc 22

A Hodder Moa Book
Published in 2009 by Hachette NZ Ltd
4 Whetu Place, Mairangi Bay
Auckland, New Zealand

Designed and produced by Hachette NZ Ltd
Printed by 1010 Printing International Ltd., China
Front and back cover photos: Photosport

Contents

List of nicknames   6

An appreciation   7

Introduction   9

Black to the future   11

Early days   17

Seven's a lucky number   36

Auckland lessons   51

Making the All Blacks   71

The 'yes' attitude   84

Professionalism   102

The Lions' roar   116

Down but not out   127

Fullbacks and centres   140

Collision in Cardiff   154

Team-mates   173

Grand Slam Diary 2008   195

Captaincy and the future   215

List of nicknames

Adrian Cashmore (Cash)
Andrew Mehrtens (Mehrts)
Brendan Leonard (Harry)
Carl Hayman (Zarg)
Carlos Spencer (Los)
Christian Cullen (Cully)
Conrad Smith (Snake)
Dan Carter (DC)
Gordon Tietjens (Titch)
Graham Henry (Ted)
Grant Fox (Foxy)
Ian Foster (Fossie)
Isaia Toeava (Ice)
Jerry Collins (JC)
Joe Rokocoko (Roks, the Rocketman)
John Mayhew (Doc)
John Mitchell (Mitch)
Justin Marshall (Marshie)
Keith Robinson (Robbo)
Keven Mealamu (Kevey, Keve)
Leon MacDonald (Rangi)
Mark Carter (Blocka)
Michael Jones (Iceman)
Neemiah Tialata (Nay)
Orene Ai'i (Renny, Rens)
Piri Weepu (Pow)
Sione Lauaki (Wax)
Sitiveni Sivivatu (Siti)
Stirling Mortlock (Stirlo)
Tana Umaga (T)
Wayne Smith (Smithy)

An appreciation

Thanks are due to many people for any success I have enjoyed in rugby. I would like to thank my mum, Ita, and stepdad, Runi Safole, for their support and understanding. It can't have been easy for my mother bringing up eight children in our extended family and I dearly appreciate what she has done for me. My older brother Faolua is another I would like to thank. He was the one I looked up to as an example, and for his support, when I was younger. They have all been very helpful and loving. I would also like to thank my dad, Fagalulu.

I would like to thank my wife Hayley who has been with me through the blackest moments of my career and who helped me get through them while also helping me a long way on the road to being an All Black. Hayley's family are also deserving of my thanks because it can't always have been easy when I was appearing in the papers for the wrong reasons. But I appreciate their love, support and invaluable advice.

I would also like to thank all my friends and the Methodist Church in Invercargill for their support through some tough days.

And my little man Max, you have been a blessing in my life and I hope that one day you will grow up to be proud of your dad.

To Lynn, your work and dedication has been second to none, and I have enjoyed walking down memory lane with you.

Introduction

Why *Living the Dream* for a book title? To tell the truth, it is really symbolic of the way my career has developed. Dreams do come true. I learnt that at an early age. I dreamt I would be the player of the tournament at a secondary schools touch tournament, and it happened. I dreamt of playing for Auckland and that happened. Then after my first game for Auckland I dreamt I would play 50 games for the blue and white hoops. I dreamt of playing for the All Blacks and I have been fortunate enough that it has become a reality.

After a test match I played in Sydney one year, my wife Hayley and I went down to the markets the next day. She had always known I used the phrase 'Dream and achieve'. We came across a stall selling tiles. There on one side of the stall was a tile with 'Dream' written on it and on the other side was a tile with 'Achieve'. As luck would have it, a little further back on the stall there was a tile with an '&', so we bought all three and they are now mounted together on my wall at home alongside my first All Blacks' jersey.

From that day on we always said to ourselves that if we dream certain things we have to push and try to achieve those goals in our lives. We've always said that, and the only dream I haven't achieved yet is winning that Rugby World Cup.

But by daring to hope and dream we have achieved many things in our lives, and this book tells the story of some of those dreams.

Black to the future

Cardiff, it's a city with perhaps the closest connections to New Zealand rugby of any city in the world. The Bob Deans try in 1905, the 1953 win by Wales over the All Blacks — the last time Wales beat the All Blacks — the Keith Murdoch incident in 1972, the Andy Haden lineout in 1978, coaching stints with the Red Dragons by New Zealanders Graham Henry, Steve Hansen and Warren Gatland, and the never-to-be-forgotten Rugby World Cup quarter-final loss to France in 2007!

Cardiff might not feature highly on the must-see lists on a British travel guide but it does have a great connection for New Zealanders, based largely on the rugby links and the temple of rugby that Millennium Stadium has become. It is an awesome venue and 30,000 New Zealanders were there on that October night in 2007. They had good cause to be happy as they pondered the kick-off. The All Blacks had gone into the hunt for the Webb Ellis Trophy as overwhelming favourites. We had played a stimulating, positive brand of rugby through the years leading up to the tournament. We felt good as a team, we were enjoying the way we were playing and we had a sense of ownership in our destiny. Our coaches had been innovative, supportive and determined in the face of some criticism. They had worked hard to produce a strong squad capable of covering any injury concerns that might hit us during such a crucial campaign. We had won the Tri Nations, we had beaten France, albeit a weakened side, convincingly in our home friendly internationals and we headed to the tournament confident in our prospects. Winning the Webb Ellis Trophy would complete the sequence of my rugby dreams.

We breezed through our preliminary games with wins over Italy by 76–14, Portugal 108–13, Scotland 40–0 and Romania 85–8. Of course, there had been some moments of interest in the build-up, the clash of uniform colours with Scotland which was a bit of a nightmare and the debate over the All Blacks' jerseys for the quarter-final with France, which was not really a concern to us, although in the final outcome it wasn't a contributing factor to events on the field.

At halftime we were up 13–3 and felt like we had control of the game, although nothing is ever certain, especially against France. We gathered in our group just before going back out onto the field and the strangest thing happened. Out of nowhere, our halfback, Byron Kelleher, said: 'This feels like 1999!' You could have heard a pin drop in the changing room when he said that. It was like he had just tempted fate. Byron didn't say the brightest things at times, but I think everyone considered that to be one of the dumbest things he could ever have said. And then we went back out for the second half.

We had started well: we were creating a lot of gaps and testing France's defences. Luke McAlister was breaking the line and getting close. But there was that middle part of the game where it just did not go our way.

It's funny when you are in a game and you know things aren't going well. No matter how hard you try, you get into this tunnel vision sort of thing where you are unable to see everything else that's going on and the different opportunities that are available. The harder you try, the worse things get. There were times in that game where we could have won it, not easily, but we could have shut them out and won.

We put enough pressure on them but we didn't convert the chances into points, apart from the time we drove over and Rodney So'oialo scored. But then we let them back in the game. There were key moments in the second half where you could feel we'd lost the game and we started to do desperate things. Lukey took a drop kick from about 40 or 50 metres out when 10 minutes before we had been right beneath the posts, which was probably the time we should have tried it. But, as I said, you've got this tunnel vision, where you are trying as hard as you bloody well can in the hope that you are going to win.

Even when the French scored that controversial try, I still felt we could do it. I had seen the forward pass. I said to touch judge Jonathan Kaplan in the in-goal that it looked pretty forward and he said, 'I didn't see it.' We knew we just had to get on with it. Our focus was to get back up there and start again. I still believe that we could have done it. It wasn't until there was about a minute or so left where there was a break in play. I was on my knees thinking 'Please no, please no'. I was hoping that it wasn't going to happen, that someone would do something special or get a try and we were going to win it, but it didn't happen.

Hearing that final whistle go was devastating. It was like the whole world had stopped. That was really hard to take. All I could think about was getting off the field. I remember the French centre wanting to swap jerseys and I said, 'No.' I wanted to get the hell out of there. I don't know what I felt, it was . . . a loss. There was no next week. You didn't know what the hell was going on. You were thinking how the heck this could have happened. It was that one moment, everything had gone into it. All the sacrifices had been made, all the training, all the work that you had done. And there it was. All taken away from you.

I suppose the way we played, we didn't click. I really don't know what it was. I remember getting off the ground and going back into the changing rooms and sitting in the showers. I didn't hear anything for ages, I couldn't. I was so upset, I just sat in there. The next voice I heard was Reuben Thorne's. I don't know how long I had been in there but he said, 'Mate, you've got to come through, Ted [Graham Henry] wants to say something', and I walked out of the showers and went into the changing room. The showers were right beside where the guys sit and all the boys were in there. I hadn't even heard any of the guys' boots walking into the changing rooms. I must have been in some other world. There was a whole group of us in the same state that I was in, and we couldn't believe it. It was a weird feeling of disbelief. Grown men were bawling their eyes out.

It was probably the hardest rugby lesson that I ever learnt that day. It was a case of having to win every single game. It was a World Cup, and there was no second chance. In some ways, it would have been nicer to have lost some of the games in the Tri Nations and to have been unsuccessful going into the World Cup. When he spoke, Ted said that he was really proud of us and he was still proud to be a New Zealander and that he loved us and we'd done everything he could have asked for. He was proud of us, he said.

We sat in the dressing room for ages, wondering what the hell had happened and why we had lost and things like that. As time clicked on a bit we started thinking about what the repercussions were going to be when we got home. It was weird. It must have taken us an age to get changed and to walk down from our dressing room, past the media and onto the bus. We heard later on that even Andrew Mehrtens, when he was interviewing one of the boys, was in tears. I felt we'd done everything right. We had done everything right off the field as well, in terms of how we behaved and treated people, how we treated our rooms in the hotels, how we had left things, and we had made an impression on people. Perhaps other people around the world couldn't believe it as well because we were the nice guys, or one of the best teams in world rugby, and this was not the way it was supposed to end.

What followed is now, unfortunately, enshrined in New Zealand's rugby history. The fact was we made our earliest departure from a World Cup tournament when beaten 18–20 by France, the tournament host, who set up this match by failing to beat Argentina in the opening game of the tournament. Yet another storm of division was inflicted on our game, and our country, as the loss was dissected and the fallout from it began. As a player the whole experience was very hard to take. Like others I had been through it in 2003. But I was young then and it was all still very new to me. This time it hurt a lot more. A lot of sacrifice by players went into that 2007 campaign but now we were out of it, after stumbling at our first significant hurdle. It may have been my last chance to seal the only missing achievement on my list of rugby dreams. I have no idea whether I will still be playing at the top level in 2011; it is still a long way off.

I still can't say definitely what went wrong. One British writer, Paul Ackford, commented in *The Sunday Telegraph* after the loss as he pondered England's semi-final against France the following week: '. . . the All Blacks actually showed England how to vanquish France last night. The

Blacks crumbled when the pressure came on at the end but when they were firing they made a mess of France's lineout and scrummage.' That just highlights how we lost our grip on the game.

We never had the chance to get together a month or two after the Cup to talk about what had happened — several of our most senior players left the side to take up contracts with clubs in Britain. We certainly didn't have the wholesale look at ourselves which occurred after the 2003 semi-final loss. I think the work we did in 2004 about setting a base for the way we wanted to operate as a team alleviated the necessity for that sort of deep exercise after 2007, and it confirmed that most of the things we had put in place were still worthwhile. Hopefully, they will continue to serve the All Blacks for their next attempt to win the Webb Ellis Trophy which, of course, happens on New Zealand soil in 2011. New players have been introduced, and more will follow, to undertake that mission.

Whether I am part of that campaign, time, form and motivation will tell. Whatever happens there is no doubt that I have enjoyed my time as an All Black, and have been fortunate enough to be able to achieve many of my dreams. Rugby has provided me with opportunities that I will always appreciate. I have had moments of regret when my personal standards slipped below the acceptable. I hope I have been able to redeem myself by letting my rugby speak for me. We are only ever caretakers of an All Blacks jersey and while I have been fortunate to become the most capped fullback for New Zealand I know that in time others will exceed my feats. My hope for them, and all others, would be that they avoid some of the pitfalls I endured, but find as much enjoyment, if not more, than I have had representing my clubs, my provinces, my Super rugby franchises and my country.

If you dream you can achieve.

Early days

Invercargill is not known for its large Samoan community, unlike Auckland. The lower temperatures are hardly an incentive for people used to living in a much hotter climate. But that was where my mother, Ita, and my father, Fagalulu, moved to from Samoa when I was three. My brother Faolua was four and my little brother Alesana was a new baby. Our parents wanted a better life for us. Mum had some family in Southland who all worked in forestry and Dad wanted to get into the freezing works down there.

Although there weren't too many Samoans in Southland, it wasn't hard to get into the local culture. But things did get tough. Mum and Dad broke up when I was about 11 and it was a messy break-up. Everything had seemed to be going well when Dad got a job as a prison officer. It was a big break for him and we thought everything was going to be a lot better than it was. But he moved away to Wellington, and I've only recently started to get into contact with him again.

Faolua and I took the break-up hard because we were at the age where we sort of knew what was going on. With Mum and us on our own it was a struggle, and we were grateful for the help we received from our church. The days that food parcels arrived were among our most exciting days as a family. I remember one occasion when we were about 13 or 14, Faolua and I were unable to afford the $5 or so we needed to go to a carnival with our mates. They said they would shout one of us but we both decided not to go. We sat in our bedroom and were frustrated at constantly missing out because we didn't have the money to go places. It was an inspiration for us to do better because we decided we didn't want to live like that when we were older. Sport became a very important outlet in our lives. Dad had been really passionate about us playing rugby, and while we played league when we were five and six, he had been influential in how we played.

I leaned a lot on Faolua. We were always competing against each other but, being one year older, he was a lot better than me. However, I strove to be like him. I was the weak little brother who got run over and cried here and there. But my brother would be the one who would make things right on the rugby field. Sport gave us boys something to do. We loved sport whether it was touch, basketball, rugby or league or whatever. We also played backyard cricket and it consumed a lot of our time and kept us out of trouble for a while as teenagers.

I played league until I went to Tweedsmuir Intermediate. I ventured into rugby simply because league died out once you got to that age. Tweedsmuir had a pretty good rugby team at the time. On Wednesdays after school we had tournaments and we used to have our inter-school tournament with Macandrew Intermediate from Dunedin. You'd never get that in league, so I suppose I looked at rugby as having more opportunities than league could offer. You only played for your league club and then played for Southland, and occasionally you might play against Otago. In the rugby environment, on the other hand, you'd play for your club and for your Metropolitan (City) team, or in a Town and Country trial game, and then you'd go on to play for Southland in a tournament. If you were lucky enough, you'd make a South Island team to play the North Island. So that's really why I thought I would stick at rugby. It also helped that I liked it a little better. There was also more rugby coverage on TV than league. And, as a nation, it appeared we were a whole lot better, if I can be frank, at rugby than we were at league.

I played for the Invercargill Club, or Blues as they are known in Southland, in the Under-58 kg level, and that was where things really started for me. I made the Southland Under-58 kg team for the annual South Island tournament and was selected in the South Island team. I played at second five-eighth, although I wasn't big at all. In fact, I was a skinny kid who anyone could run over. Picking up what skills I did have was the result of constant playing. We played a lot at home, whether it was in the back yard or on our knees in the living room every time Mum went out shopping. And we broke some things, which didn't help, including the stereo. Mum wasn't very happy. I remember every time a car would come up the driveway we'd quickly try to get the cushions back on the couch.

One of my teachers at Tweedsmuir, a Mr Norris, was pretty influential in my development. He was the head coach of the senior team. You always looked up to him and it was the goal to make it into his team. His message to us was to just get out there and give it a go. That was the thing I really took away from his sessions, to get out on the field and express yourself, and that you should go away and practise as well. He used to say not to be afraid of having a go with the ball in hand, and sometimes he'd have me playing flanker. Whether it was to get close to the ball or not, I don't know. But Mr Norris was always there. He was also the cricket coach. I tried a little bit of cricket there, but I wasn't too good.

When I was in Form Two, the All Blacks wing, Inga Tuigamala, was in Invercargill promoting his book and my schoolteacher brought him around to our house one night. We were all in bed at the time, and there would have been five or six of us there. Inga said to us that when he was our age he was always a skinny little kid with an afro. I was bemused by how thickset and big he was. So that was a special moment. We all got photographs taken with him. But I've never mentioned his visit to our place to Inga. I've been too embarrassed to say to him that I was the one of the kids in the house he visited. I don't even know whether he would remember.

I always looked up to Inga and the likes of Michael Jones, simply because of their Polynesian backgrounds. But there wasn't one particular person that I thought of as a superhero. John Kirwan was the superstar at the time, and I really admired what he did. However, being from Invercargill, I suppose I was like every Kiwi boy who dreamt of playing rugby in front of everyone.

I did feel my Samoan heritage even with so few Samoans living in Southland. We spoke the language when we came home from school, and I felt like a Samoan. When the big tours came, and the Samoan team came over to New Zealand, I was always intrigued by the following they had and was pretty proud of being Samoan. However, I was always an All Blacks' supporter. I didn't really connect with my culture until I moved to Auckland. As the years went on we'd lost the art of talking in Samoan with Mum and we'd always answer her in English. When I later moved to Auckland there were so many Samoans up there that I would speak the language often, and I really surprised Mum when I went back home by being able to speak Samoan. It's something that my brothers look at now and wish they could do. I'm quite proud of the fact that I could do that. I do pop along to the markets now and then and also go to the Pacific Days they have at schools. I'm not really keen on getting on the stage and performing, but I definitely acknowledge my Samoan background, more than perhaps I used to in Invercargill.

WHAT'S IN A NAME?

I don't know why Samoans do this. My birth name is Junior Muliaina. I've got no Malili or whatever. But I was brought up with Malili, which is my mother's uncle's name. A lot of Samoans have different names on their birth certificate to what they're actually called. But no one could really say my name Malili properly. When I visit Invercargill now everyone knows me as Malili, but they still can't say it. Even if you say Mili, or Milili, and so on. One of the players in my team down there called me Millilitres, and then my brother said, 'Oh, Mils will do.' And that's just how Mils started.

I came up to Auckland, same thing happened. The commentators couldn't say my name properly. And then as I appeared more often they asked whether my nickname was Mils, and I said yes. They said, 'Are you all right with us saying that?' And I just accepted it and said, 'Yeah, that's fine. Just call me Mils.' So that's how it stuck, and before you knew it, it was just Mils — and Malili was forgotten. To this day I still can't believe I introduce myself as Mils.

When Mum first heard it she said: 'Who the heck is Mils?' Then every time I came home she'd ask, 'Who the heck is Mils?' But I don't mind it, and it's been a lot easier than Malili, that's for sure. There are a few times when it would be nice if people just called me Malili. But Mils is unique. And it doesn't really bother me, now. Family and friends call me Malili, and everyone else calls me Mils. But there is the odd occasion when I think maybe it would have been nice to be like Josevata Rokocoko and be able to say, 'No, call me Jo.' That's one of the reasons we called our son Max, rather than a Samoan name.

While I feel that heritage, there is no escaping the fact that I always wanted to be an All Black and I think Samoan people understand that. People in Samoa love the All Blacks. They love seeing guys from Samoa, and guys born in Samoa, playing for the All Blacks. A lot of them would say that Samoa, the rugby team, is in their heart, but I think they'd be proud of what we represent and the fact that while we are in the All Blacks we are representing Samoa, the country of our birth, at the same time. And I think that makes people proud to be Samoan. People in the northern hemisphere who claim that New Zealand has pillaged the Islands to build up the All Blacks team don't really understand the situation down here. A lot of us are born here; others have come here, and often have become citizens. Many grew up wanting to play for the All Blacks. We've been here long enough and we've come for a different life, a better life, than what it is at home, and I'm purely of the view that we're New Zealanders. It's just a cold hard economic fact that New Zealand offers a better life. There would still be people in Samoa who'd say that they would want to play for the All Blacks. And they see themselves as All Blacks supporters because of the Samoans who are playing in the side.

From Tweedsmuir I went to Cargill High School. It was not long after double All Black Jeff Wilson started to make it big in both rugby and cricket. He used to visit the school, and once he was to visit to present me with a Fair Play award, which meant I would get to shake his hand and get a T-shirt and a drink bottle. But the day he was to arrive I was off sick, so I missed out. What his success did do, though, was make you think that if a guy like him could go ahead and make the big teams from a little town like Invercargill, then why couldn't somebody else do it? That was very influential. You always heard stories about the way Jeff used to practise. In cricket, he would have one wicket in the middle and just run in at full pace and bowl at it. If he missed he'd have to sprint after it and get the ball. I don't know how true those stories were, but things like that made you think, 'Wow.' Maybe if you did put some effort into things, you might get to the top level. I was always pretty keen on training hard and running and I knew, simply because I was always getting run over or because my brother was a lot better than me, that I had to work hard. I always seemed to find myself playing in the same grade as my big brother, so I knew I couldn't muscle it up every time with him and his mates. But I was always pretty keen on making sure that I learnt to hit the roads and do as many press-ups and chin-ups as I could at home. Obviously, my brother would always beat me in contests, but I accepted pretty early on that I had to train hard if I wanted to become a decent player.

Playing probably a grade above what I should have been, with my brother, was a big help. We were in the school 1st XV together for two years: he was first-five and I was second-five. We won the South Island co-ed tournament in Balclutha one year and that was massive. Brian Scott was the Cargill coach. He had coached Jeff Wilson when he scored his 66 points in a club game. So, he had a big influence on how I played.

I progressed from there, and really wanted to keep making the 1st XV. Not only did you get that different 1st XV jersey to keep but you also got your number on it, so things like that really excited me.

For all that, I did have a few disappointments while I was at Cargill, which upon reflection were really character-building. I made the Southland Under-16s and the South Island Under-16s to play the North Island, and then the New Zealand Under-16s in 1995. That was probably a year early, so I thought in the next year I'd definitely have a good chance of being selected again. But I missed out that next year in Taranaki after we played the North Island team and drew the match. I was devastated. I remember coming home to Mum. She picked me up from the airport and in the car there were tears. I told her I didn't want to play rugby ever again. She just said, 'Don't worry about it, and look ahead, you're still young.' As a 16 year old I thought it was the end of the world. Even now I get a little emotional thinking about it. I was lucky that she was really supportive, because I could easily have given it up at that time. I thought that if I couldn't make it in the second year, then, man I was a failure. It was also tough because all my peers in Invercargill had this view that I was a lot better than other kids down there, but they couldn't understand it either. In hindsight, my mother's support definitely made it a turning point in my life.

During the summer months touch rugby was my game. I think that was where my speed started to develop. I didn't realise until later that a lot of the touch I played was helping me become faster, and I suppose the game helped my skill, speed and agility. We played a lot of touch for Southland. I ended up making the New Zealand Under-18s. When I moved to Auckland I ended up in the Auckland teams as well. But Cargill High School was closing down because there weren't the numbers to sustain it. I left a year before it closed and went to Southland Boys' High School. Its rugby reputation was obviously a big pulling card. I approached the school through a friend, Phil Ono, who was a pupil there and a member of the 1st XV, which had just returned from a South African tour. Phil introduced me to Ian Baldwin, one of the coaches. Phil told Ian that I was really keen to join the school, so he said they would arrange everything for me. My thinking was that I would go to Southland Boys' for the next two years and if they were going on another tour I'd possibly stay another year.

It was a big change moving from a co-ed school to a boys' school. I was amazed at how everything was so different. They were a lot more traditional in just about everything they did. I was amazed how they prepared for their inter-schools with their caps and haka and also how the whole school got behind them. And then when you went to other schools it was a massive eye-opener to me how big a deal the inter-schools were. I found myself wondering why I didn't go to Boys' High earlier in my schooling career. I really enjoyed my time at Southland Boys', and it definitely made me a better player. I learnt a lot, rugby-wise, with Peter Skelt and Ian Baldwin as coaches. The schooling part of it wasn't so good. But the rugby was a lot more technical and they tended to be harder on you because of the greater pressure to do well. Some of those technical things in back play, like knowing how to draw and pass, made me a lot better. I remember one session we had as backs, Skelty made us train for about half an hour just diving. He didn't want us to place the ball down when we were scoring a try; he wanted us to make sure we always got the try. I don't know where he got that theory from, maybe someone dropped the ball when attempting to score or something. But we spent nearly half an hour just diving over the goal-line to ensure we got the ball down. Ever since then I've always considered that you either place the ball down with two hands or make sure you dive so it's always a try. It has been a long-lasting lesson, and something I still do today.

Practice tended to be tougher for the forwards. Skelty was always getting on top of the forward pack, literally climbing on top, and urging the guys to get a bit lower or get their grips a bit better. He had a stick and we always had to get under the stick. That was so our body positions were always lower than the opposition's. And being Southland you always learnt about rucking the ball.

Peter Skelt: 'This guy is useful'

I first noticed him as one of the younger guys in the lower-grade teams. As a 1st XV coach you always look at the younger guys coming through. I thought to myself, 'This guy is useful.' It was his balance and timing that first caught my eye. He was at Cargill High School and was king of their roost, a bit like Jeff Wilson who had been there before him. He came to Southland Boys' High School in the fifth form and had a bit of an awakening. It was a little different and there was more intensity to the training and to the commitment. He was now in a recognised 1st XV that was well thought of throughout the country and which had good results from its traditional games. It was a bit of a shock to him.

But he did have an excellent work ethic and he was always looking to improve himself. He thrived in that atmosphere, and it was a period in the school's team when he was surrounded by some pretty good players.

I remember when we went to the Top Four tournament and were taking part in the money-raising activities they have. There are four areas in

---

which the schools competed for prizes worth $500 in sports equipment. One of the contests was against a scrum machine that measured the strength of the scrum. Wesley College was one of the teams and it had some huge players, gigantic kids, most of whom were much bigger than our guys who were basically European pit ponies by comparison. We were last up. Clarke Dermody [2007 All Blacks prop] was in the team at the time and he just said to the guys, 'Here we go boys', and they hit the machine and smashed the opposing sides and we were $500 up. Another contest was a sprint. We couldn't work out who to put up when someone suggested Mils. He wasn't very keen. He was so quiet and shy, but we convinced him and he ended up winning that so we were another $500 up. There was a goal-kicking session and we got into the last two of that but lost.

Mils worked hard on his skills. We did a lot of that work in the team environment and he was a leader in the skills development, but he also did a lot by himself. We played him always at centre. He had outstanding acceleration. Over the first five to 10 metres he was superb. He had a lovely step and swerve. And with those skills at that level, that puts you ahead. He also had good timing. You can improve speed but you can't coach it. Mils also had a good game sense for rugby. Often he just popped up in places at the right time, something that other guys didn't do, and you just thought, 'That was great.'

He was gifted, but he worked at it. He had a solid upbringing, almost regimented. However, when he went to the Top Four tournament it was obvious he had the potential and his uncle enticed him to Auckland. We were disappointed. We had a team that we thought could win the Top Four the next year.

Having played test rugby I can appreciate that 1st XV games would be like test matches for most players. It's such a massive build-up. You would meet at a certain time in the hall. We played Otago Boys' in my first inter-school and you got your jersey numbered for the year, depending on how you went. The guys with the caps, they were up the front because they would be led out with the school emblem. Before you did the haka, the leader of the haka took the caps off. The whole school would be out there performing the school haka behind us as we played. I was so blown away with how it all worked and the rugby traditions. And you carry them right through to the All Blacks. I never once thought about the traditional side of rugby until I went to Boys' High. It made me love my rugby, and as far as I was concerned I really wanted to stay in the 1st XV. I was in Form Six at the time and I wanted to keep striving to be better.

After what had happened when I missed out on that New Zealand Under-16 team, Mum realised she had to be a little more supportive of me, so she started coming to my games. She had always thought rugby was a brutal game and she didn't want me getting into the rucks and rough stuff. But from that year at Southland Boys' I would look behind the posts and she was always just behind the fence watching. So that was always pretty inspirational and motivating too.

We made Top Four that year. We had to beat Aranui High School from Christchurch. There had been a lot of publicity on the TV news about how Aranui was doing so well. They had made the New Zealand schools' league finals and they were going to make the rugby finals as well, or so the reports said. But we beat them that year and we ended up going to Pukekohe for the Top Four. We played Palmerston North Boys' High in our semi-final, and lost. They went on to play Wesley College. During the week we were up there, I remember we went to Eden Park where we had a specialist coaching session and it was awesome. I got to meet Eroni Clarke and Lee Stensness because the second-fives and centres came together and we had a little chat. I couldn't believe I was on Eden Park and that rugby had brought me not just to Auckland but also to Eden Park with two All Blacks. I took away from their chat with us that you had to be able to kick off either foot, and that your skill levels always had to be better than your opponents.

We didn't do too well in the tournament, coming third. But all wasn't lost. As part of the tournament there were some side competitions and we did very well in those. We won a scrummaging competition, which was amazing as Southland Boys' started with the smallest pack. The other teams were huge and we were thinking, 'Oh man, we're going to get annihilated here.' They had a mechanism which gauged the power of the scrum on the hit. All Skelty's demands on the boys getting into correct positions helped because we whipped them. There was also a sprint, for which the boys convinced me to be the Southland Boys' entrant. I was pretty reluctant. When you're from Southland you don't tend to rate yourself highly because of the reputations of the guys from up north. I shocked myself by winning it.

I was never in a winning Top Four side. I played for Kelston Boys' High and we lost in the semis as well. I didn't see myself as a big schoolboy star, but I knew that I could play the game and play it very well. In one inter-school game we played Waitaki Boys' and I scored four tries. That was pretty special. But the big thing Southland Boys' taught me was that I had to work really hard to improve, and that you should never give up on your aspirations. I took a lesson from not making that age-group side. It was that you couldn't afford to rest on your laurels. You had to work hard. The Southland Boys' *Yearbook* said of my season: 'Malili Muliaina —

Centre. Extremely talented ball player. Skilful in all aspects and showed that he is able to beat players with flair and acceleration. Injury prevented him from being selected for higher honours. A great asset for 1998.'

I learnt other lessons as well. A fair bit of 1st XV partying went on and, being a little too big for my boots, I got involved too. We used to end up at McDonald's and get into fights and that was probably one of the reasons I left Invercargill. I ended up assaulting someone after a stupid incident over girls and stuff like that and a racist comment. I was under the influence of alcohol and I shouldn't have reacted the way I did. I used my fists, something I never thought I'd end up doing. I was embarrassed and felt really ridiculous about what I'd done. Being in Invercargill, everyone knew about it. They print things like that in the newspaper's court pages down there, whereas it wouldn't rate a mention in Auckland.

I was 17 and ended up in court. I had just been picked for the Southland Sevens team. I had no idea what was going on; I thought I was going to get this conviction thing. Stu Harvey, a policeman who used to play No. 8 for Southland, talked to me about how things went at court, about convictions and diversion. I got diversion, but I didn't even know what it was. I was very lucky that I was sentenced to 200 hours' community service. Some good people batted for me in court and the judge was lenient. I hadn't really done all that much. All I did was throw a punch, and my mate did most of the damage. It was all pretty hard to swallow. I think it really hit home that what I was doing wasn't right and though the rugby was fantastic, the partying and what-have-you weren't right. I was probably driving my mother crazy. I think she probably felt it was a good reason for me to experience a different life.

My brother had gone up to Kelston Boys' in Auckland the year before and obviously he could see that it would be good for me. When he came back to Invercargill, and saw I was starting to get into a bit of trouble, I think he realised that I needed to get out of there. However, he never talked to me about it. My eventual move to Auckland was a total surprise to me. I went up there for the New Zealand Under-18s touch tournament. After that I was supposed to be going home to say all my goodbyes and then return for a year of school at Kelston. And that was only ever going to be for a year. I would be staying with a family friend who my brother had stayed with, Matty Solomon. He was our touch coach back at high school. But despite the talk of me going to Auckland I thought when I got home from the touch event I would be able to persuade my mother to let me stay in Invercargill. I didn't want to live in Auckland; it was way too big and scary for me. But Matty tricked me. I finished the tournament, and he said, 'Right, I think it's best that you stay.' He went on: 'You might as well stay here and save your mother some money so she doesn't have to fly you back up here again.' I was stunned, and I couldn't say no. I knew we weren't rich. We hardly had any money at all. We were a struggling family and were helped by the church. And I couldn't say no to Matty. I did want to go home and say goodbye but I ended up staying.

Southland was very disappointed. I remember speaking to Skelty in town when word had got around that I might be leaving and he said to me: 'You know, there's a little pond here and there's heaps of little fish in it but you are one of the big fish. In Auckland, it's a bigger pond and there are heaps of little fish and you're going to be one of those little wee fish in a big pond. And that's going to be bloody hard for you if you go up there. In Southland, you're almost established as a big fish in a very small pond.' Perhaps, in hindsight, he shouldn't have said that to me because that inspired me to become better, to want to go up there and prove people wrong. It motivated me. I actually thought that people doubted my ability and what I could possibly do. It really stirred me to say, 'Hey, let's give it a shot up there.' If I wasn't going to become the school dux, and my future was probably always destined to be as a freezing worker or something like that, what was another year to experience something different? That probably swayed my decision, and the fact Mum and my brother got into me. I thought, 'What's a year away from home?' And I always intended to go back to Invercargill.

When moving to Auckland came about earlier than I expected, however, I was devastated. I couldn't believe what I was doing. When Matty said you'd be best to stay, I was shocked. And I remember getting back to his place after he'd picked me up from Unitec where we were staying, and I went straight to the room and started bawling. I sobbed for about two or three weeks. I couldn't believe I was in Auckland and I hadn't gone home. I was so homesick and I hadn't seen my mother. But deep down I knew that my mother could never afford for me to come back up, and that it probably was the best thing to do. Matty was supposed to keep me busy, and I guess he had seen the bigger picture as well. He probably knew that I would return home and not come back up. Mum was really good about it all. Although she missed me, she thought I had to try to stick it out for a year and see how it went. I ended up doing the rest of my community service hours at Kelston Boys', before the school year started. I had to clean the windows. I had to be there at 6 am to clean windows, collect all the rubbish bins and other chores. A few of my mates came to school to meet me. My brother had been in contact with them to make sure they looked after his little brother. They came round and they still give me crap to this day about how they

A friend for life. I have looked up to my big brother Faolua from a very early age.

Southland's Under 56-kg team. That's me on the left, second row from the back, while second from the right in the front row is All Blacks team-mate Corey Flynn.

I wonder if Inga Tuigamala remembers this moment in Invercargill on his book tour. He visited our house and made a big impression on me.

The selectors didn't do a bad job with this New Zealand Secondary Schools' team. I'm second from left in the third row while other All Blacks are: Jerry Collins (back row, left), Brad Mika (back row, second from right), Angus Macdonald (back row, right), Steven Bates (third row, fourth from left), Clarke Dermody (third row, third from right), Corey Flynn (third row, second from right), Aaron Mauger (front row, third from left) and, of course, our England representative, and captain, Riki Flutey (front row, centre).

The world championship-winning Under-19 team in 1999 with the back-row boys at left being Steven Bates, me, Richie McCaw and Jerry Collins.

Running into trouble against North Harbour in my Auckland debut, in 1999.

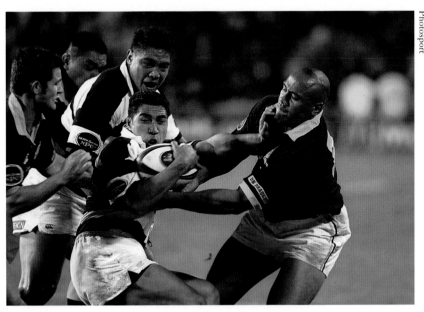

There's no mistaking one of the bigger men I've ever marked — Jonah Lomu — in this game against Wellington. Dylan Mika was there to give me a hand.

Diving for a try, just like I was taught at Southland Boys', this time against England in the Under-21 tournament at Albany in 2000.

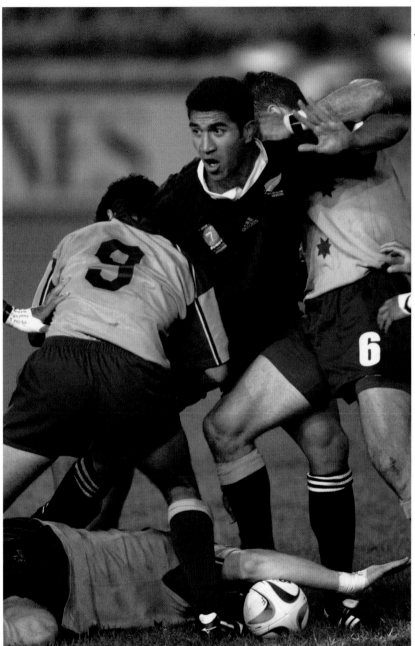

Not much room to manoeuvre here in the Rugby World Cup Sevens final against Australia at Mar del Plata in 2001. We won 31–12.

More Sevens success, this time beating Fiji in the final at the Manchester Commonwealth Games in 2002.

A moment to savour, a Commonwealth Games gold medal. Team-mates are: Brad Fleming (left), Eric Rush (second from right) and Rodney So'oialo (right).

remember me 'doing my time' washing windows and the other jobs. By late February I'd got the hours out of the way, which was a pretty good feeling.

Making the adjustment to school in Auckland was easier because of the change I had gone through from Cargill to Southland Boys'. It also helped that my brother was there the year before. All his mates were great, and they are my best mates now. I knew absolutely no one there, but they came and got me at lunchtimes and let me hang out with them. It was uncomfortable but I did it. And once sport started I got to meet new guys. I played touch in the summer, and then in the winter you got to meet all your 1st XV mates and things just progressed from there.

The transition was really smooth, although there was one occasion when my mother sent up some muttonbirds and oysters. I took some muttonbirds to school, thinking that the guys would know what they were. They had no idea and when they tasted some they spat it out. I couldn't believe they would do that because muttonbirds were really expensive.

Bruce Cunningham was the 1st XV coach, with Dennis Matene. Nigel Hothem, who was also a touch coach, was the 2nd XV coach. We had a really good year with Kelston. I played with the likes of Steven Bates, Boris Stankovich, who plays for Leicester now, and who has played age-grade rugby for England. Lua Lokotui, who was down in Hawke's Bay, and Sam Tuitupou were others. There were heaps of guys who were really talented. And we had an exceptional year. We won the Auckland competition and then the team went away on a trip to Zimbabwe.

But I didn't go. Another obstacle had appeared in my path. I had to decide whether I was going to stay and play for New Zealand Secondary Schools or go on the Zimbabwe trip. I ended up staying and playing for New Zealand Secondary Schools against Japan and Samoa. I think that was a crucial decision. Matty actually persuaded me, because I dearly wanted to go on that trip. I'd never been overseas before. I think Bernie Kelly, the NZ Schools coach, was very impressed with my decision and perhaps that got my foot in the door a little, in terms of New Zealand selections.

At Kelston I played a bit at centre, but mostly wing. When we played St Paul's I thought we were playing men that day. I couldn't believe the size of them. I didn't think I was going to survive, but we won and to cap our good year we made the Top Four. I certainly experienced something different, too, in terms of the way the school got behind their 1st XV. There was tradition but it was a different tradition. At Southland Boys' there was the likes of performing a haka, whereas at Kelston they got the rubbish bins out and started beating them with sticks and chanting or singing. I'd never experienced anything like that in my life. It was a Polynesian thing. At halftime you'd see guys running out and dancing while the drums were beating. We never had dancing and chanting in Invercargill, which was more conservative and traditional. In Auckland, the Islanders were just out there. I couldn't believe some of the things I saw.

While I was concerned about how I would do in the Auckland schools' scene I probably played a lot better than I thought I would. Matty was a big influence. He really got the training habit into me. He spent a lot of his own money taking me to a gym before school for sessions. He always used to read up on what trainers like Jim Blair and Lee Parore were up to. Matty had no background in that whatsoever but he was an intelligent man, and he always took me to the gym in the mornings. He would knock on my door at 5.45 am ready to go. I had no choice; I just got up and went with him. And he'd be my gym trainer. I remember going down to Club Physical and seeing the likes of Troy Flavell and

Ron Cribb there, training hard out, but they did so without a trainer. And here I was, a nobody who just went to school, with a guy telling me how to do this and do that. I was a little embarrassed about that, but it definitely paid off. We also did runs up in the Waitakeres and we would run up the stairs.

By the time it got to the 1st XV trainings and the 3 km time trial, I was exceeding myself. I probably opened a lot of people's eyes, and I definitely excelled a lot more than I did in Southland. Making the Northern Regions and New Zealand Secondary Schools definitely established that. I knew then that I'd gotten somewhere, finally.

Seven's a lucky number

Sevens played a big part in my early rugby development, but I have always felt a tinge of guilt about what could have been one of the biggest moments of my sevens rugby career. It was at the first IRB Sevens tournament staged at Wellington's Westpac Stadium in 2000. I had been part of the team for a few years and was heavily influenced by the coaching methods of Gordon Tietjens, a legend in the sevens game. I have never mentioned this incident before. It did teach me a very big lesson, something that has been of benefit subsequently, but which has nagged at my mind for years.

Part of Gordon's exacting regime related to what we ate. We were always on a strict diet. But the night before the finals Jonah Lomu decided he wanted to have a feed of KFC, and being Jonah you would always listen to him. But KFC was just a no-no for a sevens guy. You weren't even allowed to have ice cream. Anyway, Amasio Valence, Jonah and me took one of the courtesy cars and went to KFC. I hadn't had it for so long and, with Jonah having it too, I thought it was all right. To this day I look back and say I should have really sacrificed that trip to KFC in order to come away with a win. We lost to Fiji and in some way I put it down to that lack of sacrifice the night before.

I scored in the final. I made a break and passed it, and it came back to me somehow and I ended up scoring the try. But I was blowing and I'd never blown like that before, or after. I think it was just before halftime and the score might have been locked up, 7–7. I thought afterwards that the KFC may have been the cause of me blowing so hard and perhaps contributed to me getting so fatigued. As a result, I have never deviated from my dietary plan again. Never. I learnt a big lesson about sacrificing things, not only for myself but for the team. I thought I had let the team down. I think that was the point where I learnt that it wasn't about yourself. Well, it never is about yourself when you're playing. You've got to sacrifice things like that to get the best out of yourself, and for the team.

I got involved in sevens in Auckland when I was included in an Auckland Marist team to go to the Samoan Sevens in Apia. John Ah Kuoi was the coach, and as a result of our effort in that tournament I was selected for the Manu Samoa Sevens team. It was at the end of my last year at school. I was 18 and I ended up going to three tournaments with Samoa. It was in the days before the World Sevens circuit was established, but we went to Uruguay, Chile and Argentina. Steve So'oialo and I were the only players from New Zealand in the side; the rest were from the Islands. Steve and I hung out together. We didn't really speak Samoan that well. It was an eye-opener because the other guys had lots of prayer meetings, as well as a prayer in the morning and also in the evening. I'm pretty religious but I didn't realise how big it was in a team environment. And I didn't really know any Samoan hymns. It was different from anything I had experienced. Once we got to know the Samoan-based boys they were really good and occasionally you'd have the odd drink after a tournament which always helped. And there were some guys in there, like Semo Setiti, who had something of a background in New Zealand rugby who helped us out and we got on well with them. The experience added to my understanding of my culture.

In Uruguay, I think we might have won the plate or something like that. In Argentina we ended up losing to New Zealand in the quarter-finals, and in Chile we lost to New Zealand in the final. I played in all those games. I felt slightly odd playing against New Zealand. I knew some of their guys, and I had always wanted to play for New Zealand, but there I was playing for Samoa. I wasn't sure what the consequences might be for my longer term future. Matty found out how it all worked: because I was still at school and under 20 it was all right to play. I suppose it was a chance for me to get out onto the world stage. I didn't know anything about contracts then. It was just the chance for some exposure and to travel.

After the Chile tournament I had been promised a trip with Samoa to the next tournament, in Sydney. But about a week later I got a phone call to say that I wasn't included, instead they were going to choose guys from the island. I was a bit annoyed about that but Niko Palamo told me he had a suspicion that New Zealand would be interested in me. I went and played in the Taupiri Sevens in the Waikato and Gordon Tietjens came up to me after that tournament and asked me where I was at with Samoa. I said to him that they'd just told me that I wasn't going to be going to Sydney. So he invited me along to a New Zealand training camp which was being held just before the French tournament in Paris. That was awesome; I couldn't believe it was happening. Firstly, I couldn't believe that Titch came up and talked to me about it and, secondly, that he wanted me to go to the training camp. I was just beginning my first year out of school. I was only 18 by two or three months.

Titch's training camps are legendary and I learnt why when I went to my first one. I hadn't been worked so hard in my life. It started with the fitness testing, the beep test, the speed and the shuttle tests. At the end of the first day I got back on the bus and my head was spinning. I tried to hold on as best I could. They always said that if you were new, Titch was going to break you, and I was on the verge of breaking. I remember someone yelling, 'Stop the bus.' He rushed off the bus and started chundering, and if it hadn't been for him I would have been the one running off the bus. Titch would have broken me. It was that close. That first day just blew me away and then I had to think about being ready for day two. I honestly couldn't wait until it was all over. It was tough. We spent three or four hours out there on the training pitch. Then you'd do your recovery, head back to the hotel and know that you had to be out there to do it again the next day. It was bloody scary. And exhausting. That first night I went straight to bed because I knew the next day was probably going to be worse.

I wasn't going to quit. I always knew it was going to be hard, but I definitely had the drive to get through it. Just being in camp with the New Zealand Sevens team was motivation enough, but I never in my wildest dreams imagined that I would get called in to go to Paris. That was one of the highlights of my career. I was always going to take something away from the camp, because I was with one of the top coaches in New Zealand and one of the best sevens teams in the world, and it was quite exciting. I felt Titch would select the guys who had been there before. He announced the team in his own room. Everyone went in and sat down and he gave a little spiel before naming the team. And I couldn't believe my name was in there. I was just so blown away. And then it was off to Paris.

Orene Ai'i ('Renny') was in the team. He and I got told off in Paris for being late, despite the fact it was only by a couple of seconds. We were late to the lift where we were supposed to have a meeting before we went to training. And, sure enough, Titch got into us at training, called us all in again and said, 'Right, bloody Milly and Renny, bloody been late to training now. We're on the line and we're going to do this fitness drill.' This was my first real taste of discipline from Titch. But we had an awesome tournament and we won. It was fantastic. It was also my first real taste of being in one of the top New Zealand teams, and I quickly realised it was something I always wanted to keep doing.

I had been to South America, but Paris was something else. We did the usual things and went to see the Eiffel Tower and other sights. It was great just to be there and to experience the different language and culture, and the art. It was weird. A lot of time was consumed in training — and sleeping, because you were just so knackered after training.

In all, I think I played about 12 tournaments. I went to the first Wellington one, and Hong Kong. It was like getting a taste in miniature of what the All Blacks went through and the pressures they face, and the support and expectation — lots of New Zealanders got behind us and were always at trainings. Meeting Jonah Lomu and Christian Cullen was just massive. They were like gods to a young rugby player like me.

I enjoyed the Wellington tournaments and I think they were the best. On the other hand, Hong Kong was pretty special because if you were a sevens player it had the most history of any tournament And everyone can remember some of those tries Christian Cullen scored from the inside of his own 20, and even from behind his own goal-line. While you wish to achieve those sorts of things when you are a youngster, I still never thought I'd get there. We never had the out-and-out superstars, but we performed really well as a team. We worked hard together and that was important because it's a three-day tournament. It was one of the highlights of my career to go to Hong Kong and to win it, and to experience what other All Blacks had been through was fantastic. And to play against the likes of Waisale Serevi. Serevi was a magical player and he and Eric Rush have been the two best sevens players to date, I believe.

We had good systems in place. We always knew that if I got stepped, there was someone on the inside who was going to clean up for me. Or, if I was going to break, or someone else was going to break, someone was going to be right on our shoulder to help out. That's the mentality Titch had instilled in us. We never actually spoke about how we were going to contain players like Serevi. We were always so team-orientated in what we did that things like that didn't matter to us at all. I definitely believe that's what got us through. We were a really hard-working team; we wanted to work hard for each other, sacrifice things for each other and get the results for each other. That's probably why we were so successful that season.

After Hong Kong we headed to Japan, where I suffered a stress fracture in my foot. I had to stay over there and I got really down about it. You look back on it and think that it's kind of silly, but getting that emotional about how you've missed out and can't play was purely because I felt I was letting the team down. That was sort of the mentality we had in the group, and although it was uncontrollable you still felt that you had let the guys down because you couldn't get out there and help them. So, I ended up missing the Paris leg that year. But all that aside, it was a very memorable year and we won the series.

In 2001 it was World Cup year for sevens. The World Cup was a different type of tournament, as you would expect. The big man, Jonah Lomu, came over to Mar del Plata in Argentina for that. When he first played he wasn't going too well and we were actually starting to think twice about him. There was still the respect for him but we were concerned that he wasn't the Jonah of old. It was almost like he needed something to snap him into gear.

As the tournament advanced we were slowly starting to pick things up. But in fairness you could easily have thought from the way we were playing that we were not going to win the World Cup (or the Melrose Cup as it is called). We went through that first day with wins over Spain (26–7), Japan (52–0) and Zimbabwe (47–0), but on day two, after we beat Chile (33–0), Eric Rush damaged his knee in our game against England (17–7). He was carried off on a stretcher. At the end of the day we went back to the team motel and learnt that he was going home the next day. That was a massive blow for us. Rushie had done so much for our careers, and he was an inspiration and a great leader. To have him leave in a wheelchair for the airport was very emotional. It is the usual thing that if you are leaving the tour that you perform the haka, but obviously Rushie was incapable of doing that. So the team broke into a haka to send him on his way.

Well, you should have seen Jonah the next few games. Man, did he step up. We couldn't believe the transformation. This was the Jonah we all wanted to see. He had really flicked a switch, and just took the games by the scruff of the neck. Our first game on the last day was against Samoa and we won that 45–7. We beat Argentina in the semi-final 31–7, which was quite an experience, being on their home ground. The atmosphere was unbelievable — their music, the fans — they're all pretty crazy, and mad about supporting their team, as we know from their soccer. All those things combined to make that game the highlight of the World Cup for me. Jonah had only scored one try, against England, to that stage of the tournament, but he crossed against Argentina for another. Then we played Australia in the final. We chucked the ball to him twice in the first few minutes and he scored each time. It was awesome. He ended up with three in the game, with Amasio Valence and me scoring one each for a 31–12 win. Jonah's play on that last day was outstanding, and to win a World Cup, well, to a young player back then that was the closest thing to actually winning the Webb Ellis Trophy.

The Melrose Cup may have been a very small trophy but to win it was unbelievable. I was very fortunate to achieve that success. In fact, I didn't realise until after we had won how close I had come to not going to the World Cup. Titch told me that when he was picking the team the last place in the side came down to a choice between me and Justin Wilson. What he did was set up groups of three to have races. There was Brad Fleming and Karl Te Nana and obviously Jonah was there. We had to race over 20 metres and 40 metres, and I won both my races. Titch told me that was what clinched my place in the team. I remember racing the big man and beating him as well, so I was pretty chuffed to be able to do that. I wasn't in the best shape going into that tournament. But I did a little work and, ironically, I had concentrated on my speed. I don't think Titch realised that the bit of work I did do was all on speed. He probably wanted me to do more fitness stuff, but I tried to become faster and that obviously helped me in the end. There wasn't much in it — I only beat Justin by something like half a metre.

The Commonwealth Games came around in 2002. Just to be in the Games Village and experience something different and see all the athletes there was special. I met the likes of Irene van Dyke and Jenny May Coffin. Apart from the netballers and the hockey players there were stars like Sarah Ulmer and Hamish Carter. The team had won in Kuala Lumpur in 1998 and I wanted to go and do that in Manchester in 2002.

I'm very proud of the gold medal we won but I don't have it on show. Hayley has it stored somewhere. When I brought it back I always planned to frame it with my jersey, but I just haven't got around to it. It is special, but it was just one of those things that you want to achieve, but once you've done it, it is a case of 'What's next?' Achieving the goal was more satisfying to me than keeping on looking at the medal on the mantelpiece to remind me of what we did.

A lot of that success obviously comes down to Titch. He's got good sense for really relating with players. You have the utmost respect for many coaches, but you wouldn't have a chat or joke around with them. But Titch was great. He was your mate as well as your coach. He may have been the guy who barked orders at you and you really respected him for that, and for what he had achieved as a coach. But off the training pitch it was easy to get on with him. He joked around with you, he played dumb little games with you, and you laughed about it. But there was always that respect, that once it came time for training or if we were talking about the game, you'd value what he had to say and you'd listen. You got on with him just as you would with a team-mate. He would give as much to you as you would give for him. I think that is a quality you definitely have to have as a coach. And that's why I think the players trust him. He's prepared to be a little vulnerable in that aspect of his coaching, but he knew that when it came time to get down to business you were ready to do that for him. It's the sort of quality the All Blacks coaches have now. And because of that they are able to get a lot more out of the guys.

Gordon Tietjens:
'He's a coach's dream'

It was at the Taupiri Sevens when I saw Mils first. I was struck immediately by his skill levels and his passing. He had a lot of talents that I felt would suit the game of sevens. I spoke to him afterwards because I had a feeling that when he was younger he had played for Samoa.

I was very, very keen to have him. His passing skills were superb. He never made any mistakes. He was a lovely, humble guy, quiet and reserved like a lot of the players with Island backgrounds. He didn't show a lot of emotion at the time.

He was great, the attitudes he had were certainly going to be good for us. When he went to Super 14 and we were choosing the team for my first World Cup he had to have a race-off with Justin Wilson because they had both put on weight and we had to decide with a race who would be included.

Mils in that World Cup was brilliant. Every day he got better and better — that's the sort of player he is. He is a hard worker and he trains hard. He quite often goes to sevens training sessions when he is training with his Super 14 sides to keep his fitness up. Sevens is a great way for him to prepare. He became one of those players you always wanted.

I used him as first receiver because he gave you pace with his distribution skills. He has pace and sound vision and he's very, very smart with it.

He has got lovely handling skills. It is natural talent, you can't coach that.

He gives you time and he never panics. He's cool like the Fijians, that's what they do, create time.

He was a first-string player in Manchester and it was really great that he was able to win a World Cup and a gold medal. That was the pinnacle for him and it was very special.

It's no surprise he has done so well. He has been both New Zealand's top fullback and top centre. Even now, we haven't seen the best of him. He's a coach's dream because he produces consistent performances and he always empties the tank for you. You can't ask more than that. He sets high standards for himself and is a great team man.

What makes Titch's job tougher as a coach is the lack of time he has compared to a fifteens coach. In fifteens you've got 40 minutes to turn a game around in the second half, but in sevens you've got 10 minutes in the second half of a final to get things right, so you have to be right on the mark in your assessments. That's where I think Titch knows the game really well. You'll come together at halftime and he'll already have notes down and will say maybe the most simplest of things, like 'When we get to the ruck, just wait there a bit longer until we're settled a bit, right?' Or, 'You're not working hard enough to get to the far side to be able to collect that.' Or that I wasn't deep enough in the pocket to be able to have that release. That's a quality Titch has, being able to read what is going on in the games and to have players respond, 'Oh yeah, he might be right there, let's try that.' That's why I think he's a bloody good coach, because he obviously knows the game but he says what he knows in the least amount of time. And he's really motivating. He knows that you can do it and he has key phrases like, 'Training's a lot harder than this. We can score, we can score.' Or, 'Work harder.' When he says things like that you think about the training times you've had where it has been a lot harder than perhaps the game has been, and you know you can push it that bit further.

I believe his training sessions are slightly easier these days, but when Super 14 players came back into the squad we really used to dread it, because those guys were not as fit as us and he had to work them harder to get them up to scratch. Jonah or Cully would come back and it would be early morning sessions galore. We got up at 7 am, had a session then had breakfast, and were back on the training pitch at 9 am, so that was really tough.

Despite not knowing about our KFC episode in Wellington, Titch generally had a happy knack of catching you out when you thought you were getting away with something. Before the sevens tournament at the Commonwealth Games in Manchester we went to Liverpool. It may have been Anthony Tuitavake's birthday. Anyway, we brought out a cake and sang 'Happy Birthday' to him at lunchtime, then we thought we were going to get some of the cake. But Titch said, 'No, take that cake away' and we all groaned. Anyway, we went into Liverpool and went for a wander. We were really dying for an ice cream, which was on the dietary no-no list. It was a nice day, and the guys went and bought some ice creams and were eating them. I wasn't one of them, I have to say. And sure enough while they eating them, Titch had gone around a back street and then walked himself around, and by the time he came back he caught the guys eating ice creams.

Titch always had an inkling when guys were going to do something. At Auckland Airport when we were about to leave, he'd go through Customs first and then guys would wait until he'd gone through and would go to McDonald's and have some breakfast or something like that. I don't know what Titch would say to the Customs people but he would come back through and check what guys were up to and catch them. And the ice cream case was another example. Rodney So'oialo, Anthony Tuitavake and Amasio Valence got caught. And Titch wasn't happy about it. He let Rushie know, and we had a team meeting with Rushie. Titch wasn't there but Rushie said how annoyed Titch was. Rushie said he felt the guys needed a little bit of a treat, and that was probably one of the few cases where Titch perhaps eased off a little bit. But Rushie did tell us we had to front up the next day and make sure we performed at the tournament, because Titch was going to thrash us the next day for eating ice cream.

Any talk about the New Zealand Sevens team though has to include Eric Rush. He helped create the inclusive atmosphere that developed around the team. You felt welcome straight away. His method was to mock you, and make fun of you in order to get to know you a bit more. He always had something on you. I don't know whether he got it off other people or what, but he always had something on you so that you wouldn't know what he knew. Although it might have been something stupid or funny that you did you were still impressed that he actually took time to find out these trivial things about you. If nothing else he cared a lot and he actually still had that hard bugger in him that a lot of guys back in those days had. There were times when he would come in if there was a scrap going on because he wasn't going to take any crap from the opposition. I found that out in the Wellington tournament once when we played Australia. I had nothing to do with the fight that was going on, but I knew that if I didn't climb in there and help out, I'd probably get a bloody earful from the likes of Rushie. But for a guy who was much older when I was there, he had high fitness levels and was always beating guys who were much younger than him. You always wanted to be respected by him.

I think there was one occasion where we had fitness testing, in Palmerston North, where it was the first time he got beaten. We had to do three one-kilometre runs. Obviously, the forwards went first and the backs had to go second. Rushie was always the winner; he always won everything. But there was this guy, I can't remember his name, from Manawatu, and he beat Rushie by 30-odd metres in the first race. And we were onto him. 'Oh, Rushie, Rushie, there's this guy here, he's going to bloody . . . he's got you!' He was like, 'Nah, nah, I'll get him the next one, I'll get him the next one.' Sure enough, the next one came around and Rushie was beaten by about 10 metres this time. And we told him: 'Oh, yeah, you've closed the gap a little now.' Rushie came back: 'Nah, I've got him, I've got him, there's one more, there's one more.' And in the next one the Manawatu guy beat him again, this time by a couple of metres. And we couldn't stop laughing. 'Oh yeah, good on you, Rushie, you're gone mate, you're getting too old.' But he replied, 'Oh, yeah, yeah. Yeah, he can maybe run around the track, but can he play rugby? We'll see tomorrow.' And sure enough, the next day, Rushie certainly got the better of his Manawatu opponent.

Rushie was a great guy like that: you could always have a decent joke about what happened. You respected him because he was an All Black and one of those guys who led by example. He wouldn't ask you to do something if he wasn't prepared to do it himself. I suppose that was why he'd say, 'If one guy's in, everyone's in', and things like that. He was also much fitter than most, because he knew that if he could get himself to that level, there was no reason why guys who were a lot younger than him should not be able to do it.

Apart from all the obvious enjoyment I had from playing in those sevens tournaments, the game itself gave me a great fitness base, and it probably made me mentally resilient. I learnt I could take my body to a different place and be a lot fitter than what I had been. That attitude of being a lot harder upstairs when times are really tough, and you know that you are stuffed and you feel like there is nothing else you could possibly give, comes in very handy when you realise that the guy standing opposite you is feeling a lot worse than you are. The other aspect of that supreme fitness is that your skill level under pressure, and while fatigued, goes up 10 notches in sevens. It was similar with passing. I wasn't that great at passing before I played sevens, but I certainly became a whole heap better than I was. I definitely felt a few aspects in my fifteens game were improved as a result of playing sevens.

Auckland lessons

By the time I finished my year at Kelston, it is fair to say there was a reasonable amount of interest in Southland about getting me to resume my rugby career down there. I still missed home. I had been existing on a student allowance granted for living away from home. That was worth about $100 a week, of which $50 went on board. I could talk all I wanted on the phone after 6 pm with my mother, or my friends, down south. And I did that quite often.

Southland offered me $10,000 for an NPC (Air New Zealand Cup now) contract. To me, barely out of school, that seemed like millions. Matty, the guy I boarded with, and I spoke about it a lot, discussing all the pros and cons. With Southland chasing me, Matty rang the Auckland Rugby Union's development officer, Steve McHardy, to tell him what was happening. Steve jacked up a meeting with Ted (Graham Henry), himself and me. Ted didn't know me at all at that stage or anything about me as far as I knew. When he heard what Southland was offering me he sort of laughed, and then I thought he was joking in that sort of dry manner he has when he said, 'Sign him up. Sign him up with an NPC contract for Auckland.' He wasn't kidding. They offered me two grand tops, but money wasn't the issue.

Before I made a decision, I returned to Invercargill. I didn't really want to make anything of what was happening in the background, but I went in the door at home one day and my mother and brother were sitting at the table. That told me there was going to be a serious talk about the situation. I didn't know it at the time but my flight back to Auckland had already been booked.

We sat down and they told me, strongly, that I should go back to Auckland and give it a go. I was pretty upset and practically begged my mother not to do that to me. Finally, after much discussion, my brother said to me: 'Look, I mean no disrespect to the Southland guys, but who would you rather run out of the tunnel with — Simon Culhane or Michael Jones?' That ultimately was the deciding factor. And within a year I was living that statement. Not only did I meet Michael Jones but I ran out of the tunnel at Eden Park with him. While the decision to sign with Auckland was bloody hard, at the time it was the best thing I could do for my career.

Even when I was living in Southland, Auckland always had my admiration for the way they played and they were my favourite team. Players like John Kirwan, Michael Jones and Eroni Clarke all made big impressions on me. It also helped that in those days Auckland were always so successful. It was funny how things turned out after my meeting with Ted. I went back to Invercargill for a brief visit before returning to Auckland with the decision made to sign up. Amazingly, I had only been in Auckland a month when Ted up and signed as Wales' coach! But I took on the Academy contract and joined up with the Suburbs club. Being in Auckland and playing senior club rugby was a huge stepping stone for my future. Having signed for the Academy for two years and then getting involved in a club made it easier to handle staying in Auckland. Eroni was there and Blocka (Mark Carter), Craig Dowd and Rico Gear. A lot of my mates went to the same club and so did some guys from school. I knew I had a couple of years there and I really enjoyed it. It helped that we made the semis in the first year, and Tony Hanks, who is now the Waikato coach, was part of the Suburbs crew. I knew him from school because he visited Kelston quite a bit.

I really enjoyed the club scene. I think probably more so because of the partying afterwards and then drinking at the clubrooms. We made the semis of the Gallaher Shield competition but lost to Ponsonby. We scored in the last few seconds and we were up by three or four and then Ponsonby came back and scored on fulltime. It was disappointing but I really enjoyed that level of rugby. Bruce Birtwistle was the coach, with Shane King. It was a bit different to the only other final I had played. That was when I was a schoolkid at Kelston and I was asked to go back to Invercargill by Star to play in Southland's big club final for the Galbraith Shield final.

I played wing for Suburbs, and I think that's when Grant Fox and Wayne Pivac looked at me. The first time I played for Auckland they thought they would play me at fullback. I didn't know anything about fullback. I'd once played in that position for the New Zealand Under-19s when Shannon Paku was injured, but that was all. I had been picked to attend an Auckland camp from Suburbs in 1999. I had started the year away with the New Zealand Under-19s at the world championship in Wales. We won that tournament by beating Wales 25–0 in the final.

Earlier we beat Romania 63–15 and Ireland 21–15. There were a few names in that team that would be prominent later. They included Riki Flutey, Aaron Mauger, Isaac Boss, Jerry Collins, Clarke Dermody, Campbell Johnstone, Richie McCaw, Brad Mika and Tony Woodcock. After that I played in the Paris Sevens tournament. There was a game for the New Zealand Rugby Academy against the Australian Barbarians when I came on as a substitute for Mark Carrington.

On 3 August 1999, I made my first-class debut, for Auckland. They put me at fullback because Adrian Cashmore was injured. It was also Xavier Rush's blazer game and I remember him going on about actually receiving his All Blacks blazer before he had an Auckland one. I got knocked around a bit in that game. When I made a tackle on Rua Tipoki he kindly stuck his forearm into my mouth. I needed to go off for some stitches because I had bitten through my lip. I also suffered a bit of concussion.

It was after that game, in his after-match speech, that Wayne Pivac said he thought I had a big future. I didn't take too much notice of it at the time — I thought it was just another coach's spiel. But in looking back it was quite a special time for me because I had never thought I would play for Auckland. I was picked for another game down in Blenheim, but they didn't make me a permanent member of the squad until Michael Jones' farewell game for which I sat on the bench. Before the end of that season I was selected for the New Zealand Under-19 team to play Australia. We lost to them 16–20.

My year in 2000 gave me a lot of sevens rugby, but I also played in an international Under-21s tournament held in New Zealand, which we eventually won, beating South Africa 71–5 in the final. I had 10 games for Auckland on the wing in the NPC, which we lost when going down to Wellington 23–48 in the semi-finals.

The big step came in 2001. I was included in the Blues squad for the first time. I got on the field as a substitute in the first game, against the Highlanders, started the next two games then didn't play again until the last round. Adrian Cashmore, who had been the Blues fullback, left Auckland that year and in a discussion with Foxy he thought they would look to play me at fullback permanently. I had been playing wing for the NPC team in 2000 and I was a little taken aback. I honestly didn't know anything about fullback. And it was a bit scary, to be honest. The first couple of times I'd played there I felt I was in no-man's land out there at the back and not really doing anything. But Foxy must have seen something because he said that he thought I had a big future and that one day I'd wear the black jersey. Coming from Grant Fox, who was a legend, that had me wondering, because I'm not one of those people who thinks too highly of himself. I knew it was going to be challenging, but it turned out well. I played nine games in the NPC at fullback and finished with two on the wing. I didn't really get a lot of tuition about how to play fullback. I took note of Cash.

I used to watch him in trainings to see what he did. And I was helped a lot by Doug Howlett. I found you had to have really proficient wingers who could assist, and Doug was influential in that. He helped me greatly with things like positional play and not having to worry about covering the whole field. That was a big lesson because finding myself back there I was really worried about how I could look after what seemed to be such a massive area of the field. But to have someone like Doug say, 'Look, don't worry about this end, you cover that other half and I've got this half covered' was great. That put me at ease. I also picked up a lot of tips from watching games.

Grant Fox: 'a real feel for the game'

I remember first watching Mils play out in the windswept middle of Avondale Racecourse for Suburbs. What we saw was a guy who was well-balanced, had good pace, good footwork, a really good feel for the game and an understanding and anticipation of just where he needed to be. It was an innate thing, a real feel for the game.

We were well covered on the wings with Doug Howlett and Caleb Ralph and here was a guy with a skills set who could play fullback.

It was not something you see often in players of his age. He had a rare talent that even at his young age suggested that, boy, this kid could really develop. You could sense he had that something that marked him ahead of most of his peers.

You wouldn't say that he was that much better than everyone else, but every once in a while you do identify someone who is gifted and he looked like he was.

The only flaw that I ever saw was that he didn't have the strongest kicking game. He's developed that really well, but at the time it wasn't a strong suit. He had all the other attributes, but he wasn't the strongest on the kick return.

Part of my philosophy was about picking your best players then looking at their skills to fit them into different positions. You don't do that all the time, but where you had three guys like we had it was a case of where do you mesh them.

I remember one occasion when he was on the physio's table at practice and I said to him, 'Mate, if I laid three jerseys out with 13, 14 or 15 on them, what would you pick? And he said: "15." I remember saying to him: I think you would make an outstanding 13.'

I still do. While he is absolutely world-class at fullback, I think given time regularly in the 13 position he could have developed into a world-class 13 as well. I think he has the skills to play there as well. As he ages, he could well end up there, quite conceivably.

He came to me for kicking help and I probably didn't give him as much time as I should have, but the reason for that is you get so locked into what the team is doing that you don't spend enough time with individuals. That was one of my weaknesses. And if I did it again I would somehow make space for more one-on-one time.

Mils was one of those guys who would work on things himself. You would come to training and he would be there early. He might be taking high balls, practising his kicking or running onto the ball, the in-and-out move. He was very diligent like that. He didn't need to be pushed, he was one of these guys who, I think, saw the opportunity in front of him and who made the decision early on that he wanted to be the best that he could be and that is all you can ask of any athlete.

You like to think that you saw something that suggested he would go all the way. We saw a guy who was gifted but you don't think, 'Gee, he's going to be a superstar', as much as you desperately want them to be. We may have helped give him a break, but the rest was up to him, and he's done it. Now he's the consummate pro.

I had noticed some subtle stuff Cash did, like asking his wings to do certain things. I tried to copy him. At that stage I didn't have any idea why he did it; I just did it because I had seen him do it. As the years went on, it dawned on me why he asked his wingers to check first before they came and covered his back. It just went from there. Another thing was that I didn't kick much and that was probably the most worrying thing. Having been a centre down in Invercargill, and then a wing in Auckland, you didn't really kick a lot, and the game back then wasn't really about kicking. So the only solution was to spend more time practising my kicking. It was a few years before I felt comfortable about my kicking game. For a long time I worried about it too much — about how I was going to hold the ball for a spiral kick and so on. At one stage I got into the situation where I was thinking I had to kick all the time. It was probably 2002 or 2003 before I realised it wasn't all about kicking and that the exercise involved in thinking about kicking took away some of the love I had for running with the ball. I started to think I would try to run a little bit more and I felt a lot better. Before you knew it, I felt much more comfortable about kicking as well. You don't have to kick all the time in certain situations.

With more games for Auckland I started to gain some confidence and I felt increasingly accepted by the team. I hadn't really been part of that NPC-winning side in 1999. Although I only played the first game, they ended up ringing me to join in their celebrations, which involved everyone shaving their hair off. Junior Tonu'u shaved mine off. In 2000 we were second on the table but lost the semi-final in Auckland to Wellington. They went on to beat Canterbury in the final. It wasn't till 2002 that we won the championship again. We had to win four games in a row, after we'd been given hidings by Canterbury and Waikato, and that was when they started experimenting with me at centre. We had to beat Otago while also picking up five points and then go down to Wellington and beat them also with a bonus point. We managed that and found ourselves facing a trip to Christchurch to meet Canterbury in the semi-final. We turned around our earlier loss by winning 29–23. That set us up for the final against Waikato in Hamilton. Just as we had with Canterbury, we turned around our earlier loss and took the championship with a 40–28 win. That was amazing, just a tremendous experience.

In so many ways 2002 was a significant year in my rugby. I had some pretty good highs that year with the Commonwealth Games Sevens gold medal, the NPC title and more regular play. But I also had a massive low with a stupid incident, when I was fined and suspended for a couple of weeks by Auckland for urinating in a bar. That episode forced me to take a good, hard look at myself, my rugby and where I was going. It made me realise that I wasn't just a rugby player; I was a player with a higher profile than I realised and I couldn't carry on as I had been. While I was making progress as a rugby player I still felt I had a degree of anonymity and that I was protected in a team environment. But being plastered over the front page of the *New Zealand Herald* for what I had done really drove home to me that things had changed.

Let's be honest, urinating in bars was not something I went around doing. I look back at it now and at the time I didn't even know what I was doing, which has never been any sort of excuse. I didn't know anything had happened until the next day. I was called by our manager Derek Sampson and he said he wanted to meet with me. So I went and met him and he asked me what punishment I thought I should get. I still didn't realise then what I had done. When he explained it to me it was one of those times that you think to yourself, 'Did I actually do that?' I didn't know how it happened or where it happened. He'd obviously spoken to the senior players about it. I was naïve thinking no one would know who I was. I was forgetting the fact that it wasn't just all about me, it was about the team, and I hadn't even thought about that.

After our meeting I went out to dinner with the family that I lived with and a *Herald* reporter called their house. I couldn't believe it. I didn't know what to think. I rang Derek and said what had happened. He said he would call back but I never heard anything. I figured that things had quietened down, and it was at training the next day that I was finally able to grab the paper. I looked through the sports section. There was nothing in there. And then I folded the paper up and just as I turned it up, there was my photo, with a story, at the bottom of the front page! I froze for a few minutes. I couldn't believe it. I went and apologised to the people at the bar where it happened and they were really good about it. They said it was a storm in a teacup and if it wasn't for who I was then nothing would have happened.

That comment kept eating away at me. People were actually saying, 'If it wasn't for who you were no one would know about it.' I still didn't think of myself as someone who people would take any notice of. That attitude was immature. At 21 years old I still thought that I was back at school. But it rammed home to me that life was now different. People didn't solely look at you playing; they were also looking at what you did off the field. I was oblivious to people worrying about what I did off the field. That's why I warn the young guys about it now: 'You don't want to end up on the front page like me.' And if we have a beer I make sure they don't stay too long.

For two or three years I lived the dream of playing for Auckland. And to me that was all. I thought I'd done everything I could do. There was the All Blacks but back then it seemed like an impossible hope for me. I'd come from a small city and I was living a pretty good life. I had a couple of years where I got into the alcohol scene a bit. Back then it was almost part of being a rugby player. After a big week, which involved days of training and then the game, you'd always have court sessions before going out. Being from Invercargill, I didn't mind drinking. I was probably the only guy there with a brown complexion who drank. The other guys didn't really drink and the likes of Craig Dowd always looked after me. I felt part of that group because of the way they would say, 'Come over here, have a beer with me.' I found myself doing that for two or three years in the early part of my career. I wouldn't change what happened that night. Obviously I got myself totally intoxicated, as I always would every week. Being young, you'd recover pretty fast and get out there again and train on the Monday and the whole cycle repeated itself.

Of course, I then had to tell my mother what had happened. That was the hardest thing of all. She was devastated when I called her. I could hear the disappointment in her voice. Despite her pain, she was really supportive and she said, 'Don't worry about it, son. You know I love you.' I think she felt let down because she hadn't brought her son up like that, and certainly not to do dumb things like that. I knew she was embarrassed. Invercargill is a small town and people talk. Mum goes to church down there, and the church had helped us out as youngsters. I was only making the Auckland team then and my career hadn't really started. I knew that Mum was hurting, but her words were ones of support. It would have made me feel a lot better if she'd just come out and said, 'Son, I'm really embarrassed with what you've done.' I don't think Mum realised I drank until then either, so that probably hit a little harder as well.

That incident made me resolve never to do that to my mother again. I'm glad the way things have turned out, because I like to think that I've erased some of the bad memories that she'd had and filled them with some really good ones.

I was fined and suspended by Auckland, and I received counselling. That was a hard step to take because when you say counselling it is as if there is something wrong with you. And I didn't feel there was anything wrong with me. But I have to say that counselling helped. It made me aware of some things that I didn't even realise, as to why I was acting in certain ways. I realised how important my family was to me. I'd gone away from some of the principles our family held dear. Although I rang home, and still ring now, at that time it was just a chore. I'd help out as best I could but I'd moved away from a lot of things that I really stood for. Those sessions with the counsellor were beneficial. It was good to have someone to confide in as well — to talk about life and things other than rugby that I was struggling with. I didn't have someone to talk to about that. I didn't have a mentor who I could go to and say, 'Man, life is pretty great, and I'm boozing a lot and, maybe, I think I've made it.' I actually needed someone to say, 'No, pull your head in. You've got this massive opportunity to become an All Black.' Things had gone well for me, and in Auckland I'd been able to buy my own house. I was expected to be an adult and go about it my own way. But there had been no real steadying influence in my life.

I don't know if that is something that rugby officialdom should concern itself with. It's probably up to the individuals. I think players confide in those they trust in their team environment. As I've gotten older, I have had a lot of guys asking me for help. And perhaps I should have sought help more when I was younger. I didn't think to go to an older guy and ask for advice. You didn't want to expose yourself by asking them how to do something. There were a lot of guys who had been in the semi-pro era when I made the Auckland team. Those older players grew up when the game wasn't pro, so there were two different environments. You had to develop the attitude of those guys who'd been there the longest and that's probably where I got caught out a bit. You played hard, you trained hard, you drank hard. And if you had any problems you had to go away and fix them yourself. No one was willing to share any of their experiences and whatever mishaps they had had. Perhaps they just laughed about certain things. And I thought it was all right to keep going like that.

I think the game has changed a lot in that way. Back then, however, I always thought you weren't man enough or tough enough if you had to go and ask for help or advice. It was the same with playing at fullback. You had to do it yourself to prove to them that you were capable, or that you were good enough to play in that position. Perhaps I should have been the one to go and ask, rather than persist with the macho attitude we had in those days. The pressures back then were definitely not the same as they are now. You had to prove yourself to the seasoned pros. There was also a group, generally of players with Island backgrounds, who were quite religious. I'm fairly religious, and I went along to their prayer meetings before games. But I wasn't as dedicated as they were, and still are. Michael Jones and Eroni Clarke were the opposites of the other crew that I drank with. But I didn't feel that I could talk to them about my problems because they were such nice guys and I didn't want them knowing my issues. They were influential in my career and Eroni was one who spoke to me a lot after that bar incident.

Nowadays, it's definitely different in situations like the one I found myself in. Obviously, there are still plenty of players who find themselves in the papers for the wrong reasons. With the Internet, incidents also get exposed far more than before and you feel some sympathy with guys who find themselves in those situations. I'm not trying to condone their actions, but having had my name dragged through the papers I feel for them. But it's the guys who don't learn from their mistakes who really annoy me. If you don't learn from something like that and make it better then you might as well give up. You have to accept the fact you are in the spotlight and act accordingly.

I always feel for the young guys. These days, players start playing professionally at younger and younger ages, and they're expected to be adults. A classic example is Isaia Toeava, an All Black as a 19 year old, who probably still doesn't realise it now at 22 that he's under the microscope. But he was, right from day one when he became an All Black. People go on about how they should be role models. I don't believe that guys are role models at that age. You're asking 19 and 20 year olds, who are still trying to find their own mentors and role models, to be role models for younger kids. I've realised through my own experiences that you have to talk to young guys about responsibilities and behaviour when they go out and when they're drinking, because they need to know that if something goes slightly wrong it can get blown way out of proportion.

My incident forced me to make more sacrifices if my career was to advance. The All Blacks still seemed a dream, but something of an impossible dream. I wanted to do better for my family so that I was not being selfish and thinking it was all about me. I needed to change my behaviour. It was a massive learning curve in my career, and my first goal was deciding to finish off the year by doing everything I could to win the NPC. It was great to accomplish that. But in spite of the wonderful feeling of achievement I had some very quiet nights after that bar episode.

It is hard to describe the feeling I had when my brother made the comment about running out onto the field with Michael Jones. I had been through the unreal feeling of being named in the Auckland squad and being given a new training kit. Then out on the training field I came face to face with the legend. We were doing an exercise where guys with a ball had to try to get past four others who had tackle bags and who were trying to stop you passing them and getting to the goal-line. Being the young guy I had to be one of those who ran at the defenders. Whichever way I went two of them were going to come at me. I looked up and there were Michael Jones and Eroni Clarke on one side with the tackle bags and Junior Tonu'u and, I think, Leo Lafaiali'i on the other. I knew what side I was going to try to get by on because there was nothing surer than I was going to get hammered. I headed towards Junior and Leo. But, somehow, I ended up in the middle and, as I had feared, I got annihilated. So there was no time to get big-headed. I quickly learnt where I featured in the scheme of things.

At another training session, I remember Iceman, Michael Jones, didn't even fend me off. It was just a passive run but he actually put his hand on my chest and it felt like his hand covered my whole body. I was so in awe of him. Off the field he was even better. They operated in the Eric Rush vein of mocking you off the field to try to get to know you better. And they were very good at it. They gave me the last name of 'Pivac' and called me 'MP', simply because of Wayne mentioning in that after-match speech about the big future I supposedly was going to have. For a year or so they called me MP — short for Mils Pivac.

Bruce Robertson: 'I like him at fullback'

A couple of Auckland's rugby development officers mentioned Mils to us and said he was an outstanding player. So we went and watched him, and he was outstanding. It is rare when you see a player at that age who doesn't make many mistakes. But, like good players at that age, he stood out because he did a lot of things correctly.

His running and physical skills impressed most. We looked at him coming through our system.

On the coaching side I had a bit to do with him when he played in the New Zealand Colts side against the Blues. Mils was an outstanding person, he was always listening and he did what he had to. He was shy early on but he let his actions do all the talking for him. As he got more experienced he became more vocal.

He had to keep working on his game. You can't rely on natural ability being enough. He played around a bit, on the wing, centre and fullback. When he consolidated at fullback he had to work on his line kicking especially. It would be fair to say that Mils has never mastered his goal-kicking skills. He was quiet, but quite resilient in what he wanted to achieve. Sometimes he didn't stand out but what he did was done very accurately in terms of knowing when to pass and when to kick.

People who make good decisions, that's what you want. With the skills set he had and decision making he was always going to be either a centre or fullback. He was more valuable there than on the wing. At fullback, he made it so it was his position. I like him at fullback: he runs into the line well and makes good decisions. As he's got into the test arena he's grown at that level again. He's made it his own and does things very well. Once you saw him develop you knew he was going to be an All Black.

It was a great time to play for Auckland. Carlos Spencer was another big name in the side. You loved Carlos Spencer or hated him. If you didn't know Carlos you'd say he was arrogant and a lot of people didn't like him because they thought that. In fact he was quite shy. He was easy to get on with but I think a lot of younger guys struggled to do that. He wouldn't talk to a lot of the guys, simply because of his shyness; he found it hard to go up and say, 'Gidday, I'm Carlos', or whatever. I had a lot of time for 'Los'. He helped me a lot and we joked a lot off the paddock. On the field he was amazing. What I liked about his approach was that although we'd all concentrate so hard during the action, in the breaks in play he'd come up to you and joke about things. I couldn't get over that. Here was a guy in a key position, and so good at what he did, who in the midst of a game would start joking, or he'd come over and say, 'Oh, jeez, these forwards are bloody shit', and start laughing about it.

That's what I really admired about Los. He didn't care what people thought about him. He went out there and wanted to create new things and do stuff that no one else had done. It was his way of overcoming his shyness by using his time on the rugby field to show all his cards and let people know what he could do. I felt privileged to be able to play so many years with him. As my career went on, he would ask me on the field what we should do in some situations and I was humbled by that. There were times when he moved away from the team plan. He was unpredictable and would create something out of the blue. I got used to that. I learned that if I hung deep enough, or just waited for him and gave him heaps of space to let him do his thing, before you knew it something would happen. If I held and he went through, he was gone. You had to adapt to the unpredictability of his play. All those training sessions together and the conditioning games helped. You learned to tell when he might be up to something. There were times when it didn't work but when it did, it could be spectacular.

Los' involvement also helped me in the later part of my career, especially with my kicking. When we did skills work, a lot of guys wouldn't go and kick with him. But he would always come over and say, 'Let's have a kick.' And he'd make it a competition, in which he'd beat me hands down.

I learnt a lot about how he kicked. We would kick a big tennis ball, it was a massive one, a lot bigger than a soccer ball, and he used to always say to me, 'When you're kicking the rugby ball just imagine it's that soccer ball that we had out there, or the tennis ball that we were kicking.' And it actually worked! Los would come out of his shell if he trusted you and you had performed well on the field. Off the field he could be an amusing guy.

Doug Howlett helped me a lot with my game, especially watching the way he prepared. He was a constant professional and he still is. The way he looked after his body and what he ate and how he trained was impressive. He's one of those guys you'd look up to and copy some of the things he did — the way he warmed up for instance. He had his Is dotted and his Ts crossed. He had some secrets which he didn't give away for a long time and until I had got to know him really well off the field. We used to go out and surf and play a bit of golf and then he started giving me some of his secrets of how to get to the ball before other players. I was always intrigued how he could do that and how he got in the right positions near that sideline. Often he started further away from the ball than I did and he'd always end up first there.

I probably worked harder than Dougie, but not as cleverly as he did. I think he learnt that off Wayne Smith, because when I got into the All Blacks a lot of that came out in their coaching. It's the old story, I wish I knew then what I know now. I might have progressed a lot faster perhaps. Dougie is a good mate. We've had some good and some bad times together and he's an exceptional guy who I've got a lot of respect and time for. I still remember when he texted me after I first made the All Blacks. He said, 'You're my drinking buddy, my surf buddy and, now you're finally in, my All Black buddy.'

Rens, Orene Ai'i, was always pretty good during my time with him for Auckland and the New Zealand Sevens squad. I always sat beside him and had my cubbyhole beside him at Eden Park. Brad Mika was another player I got on well with. All those guys had a sense of humour, and they made training a lot easier. When we came off the field we were always able to have a big laugh. In Auckland, because of the Polynesian influence, you end up hanging out together. It was certainly a factor in me learning more of the language.

I thoroughly enjoyed my time at Auckland and I was privileged to be able to wear the blue and white hoops. And the day that I left was really emotional after we'd won the final in 2005. I always thought that once I'd made that Auckland team I'd never play for anyone else. But who's to say? I might play for them again. You never know.

One thing about playing for Auckland and the Blues that I realised only after I'd left was the pressure to win. That is one thing that is different about playing there, and it is probably the same for the Crusaders and Canterbury. I don't think the likes of Waikato and the Chiefs realise how heavy the pressure to win is on the likes of Auckland. I know many people see the expectation of them winning as arrogant. And it may be the biggest city thing, but they do think they should be championship winners every year. And whether they like it or not they have to put up with it. Whereas the public response is to play down the expectation of winning, the pressure within the team environment is that you have to win. In 2002 when we weren't doing so well, Gary Whetton came down after training and gave us a serve. We thought here was another former All Black who wanted to get into us. Some of the guys were not impressed. But looking back now he at least said it to our faces and stressed what being an Auckland player was about. You had to bloody win, there were no doubts about it.

On the other hand, with the Chiefs, for example, there's a great fan base. They're bloody passionate and they love their team. But whether they win or lose they're always going to be there, year in and year out. They're the most vocal supporters around. However, I sometimes get the feeling that it's all right if the Chiefs finish fifth or sixth or whatever. That's just a feeling that I've had, and I've shared that a couple of times with the likes of Tasesa Lavea, who was down there, and Sam Tuitupou. That's the uniqueness of being in Auckland. It's a given that you have to win, and if you don't you are going to hear all about it. I think it has worked in Auckland's favour to have to win year in, year out. There is no happiness if you don't make the semis and there's definitely no satisfaction at coming anywhere less than the top four.

Making the All Blacks

There have to be better ways to remember your first selection for the All Blacks than what I managed in 2003. After the Blues won the 2003 Super 14 final we had a party at the Alinghi America's Cup base in Auckland and ended up at Spy Bar. We got kicked out of the bar, not for anything I had done, it has to be said. Doug Howlett had thrown a glass at a person serving at the bar. Doug walked upstairs to where I was and told me to hurry up and come with him. I'd just come back from the bathroom so obviously I had learnt from my earlier experience! When we were leaving we did everything we were told to do. But the bouncers started giving us the verbals, so we abused them back as we kept walking. The bouncers kept following us. We jumped into a cab. I jumped in first, via the back door, and the bouncers were still going at it. All of a sudden the roadside door was opened. I turned around towards it and then I got a massive bollocking. They dragged me out of the taxi and three bouncers started laying into me.

We eventually managed to get away and I went home that night with a massive black eye which I found out later was due to a broken eye socket. The next day it was all over the papers what Dougie had done and that I had got into a scrap. It was really disappointing for me after what happened the previous year. I hadn't had a drink all season until we'd won the final. I was making a deliberate stand for all those people I had embarrassed in 2002, while also hopefully making a bid to become an All Black. I wasn't angry or disappointed at being given a hiding by the bouncers. I could accept that. I would have been mouthy. But I'd done everything to get out when we were asked to leave. In that situation you jump in a taxi and you get out of there. I would have just left it at that. But when the bouncers gave the press their view of what had happened and included a few lies, that really hurt.

The next day was Sunday and the news was already out. The All Blacks team for the first test of 2003, against England, was to be named on Monday. And here I was being portrayed as a real bad guy who always goes out on the turps, urinates in bars and then gets into fights. It really hurt that I hadn't done anything wrong. All I'd done was just mouth off at the bouncers.

I sat watching the team announcement with my black eye. My mother was there. She and Runi Safole, my stepfather, lived in Australia by then and I'd flown them over to watch the final, and then I turned up at home like this. Anyway, we watched the All Blacks' team announcement, and the coaches went through the alphabet and reached the Ms. When I first heard my name I could not believe it. Everything that had happened 24 hours before was erased in an instant. I was over the moon. I could only see out of one eye but it didn't matter. Our celebrations were short-lived, though, simply because I was in no shape to do much. But having my mother there was great. I felt I had redeemed myself somewhat for what had happened the year before. Then the text messages started coming through. My phone went berserk.

It was only later that I found out what had taken place when the news of the assault had got out. John Mayhew ('Doc'), the All Blacks doctor, had rung All Blacks coach John Mitchell. I didn't know Doc until much later, when I got on really well with him. He'd told Mitch what had happened and what was going on. Apparently Mitch laughed a little and said, 'Okay, that's fine.' I later asked Doc: 'Was there ever a stage where perhaps he said, "Oh stuff him"?' He said, 'No, it was never that at all; you were always going to be named.'

That was outstanding, but once again I had managed to make that selection another drama in my life. Being named in the All Blacks for the first time is just as everyone says it is. Hearing my name was all I could remember throughout the whole week. There were a lot of good feelings to follow that really gave me a boost.

I was fortunate through someone else's misfortune to be able to play regularly in my first year. Leon MacDonald was injured, so I got to play at fullback often and I was able to progress from there. Tana Umaga mentioned one thing to me that was really helpful. He'd said that although I'd gone through all the adversity and all the hard times, I wasn't to worry about what had happened. 'Just forget about it. You play some really good rugby and people will start to forget about all those things that have happened.' That hit home, because there was part of me that was really bitter about what had occurred. I could accept the fact that the year before was all my own fault, but this time round I'd been the innocent party and I was the one being made to look like the villain. I was still in that frame of mind, wanting to clear my name from the year before by not drinking and playing well, and then I wanted to do it again for this thing by laying charges. We tried to find who the guys were. But it ended up they couldn't find them. The videotape at the bar wasn't recording that night and I ended up dropping the charges during the World Cup.

The World Cup was in the future, though. First, we had to play England and Wales, and the Tri Nations. The squad to play England was named 12 days before the game, and we came together a week out from match day. There were a lot of debutants in that team. Rodney So'oialo and Ma'a Nonu were two. The whole experience of going into camp and all that went on was amazing. I roomed with Leon MacDonald, who told me the coaches would come around and tell the guys who weren't playing why they hadn't been picked. He warned me to try to avoid Mitch and Robbie Deans because they would try to find me if I wasn't going to be playing. Leon had been concussed in the Super 12 final and went home on the Tuesday the team was to be announced. I tried to avoid the coaches like Leon had told me.

There was a knock on my door and I thought it was one of the guys. I opened it and there were Mitch and Deans standing there. I was thinking: 'Oh no!' I didn't quite keep out of their way. But Mitch said: 'Look, you're on the bench and you're going to come off the bench. You're going to play. And congratulations.' They had decided to play Doug Howlett at fullback in place of Leon, while I was in the reserves. I was thrilled. I was going to get my black jersey and I was hopefully going to get on and play my first test as an All Black. I quickly got on the phone and rang my partner Hayley and I rang my mother. I arranged for them to fly down. I was making sure that they were both there, to witness this game. And Hayley's mother came down as well.

But as the test went on, and kept going on and on, I was looking up at the clock and time was ticking away. When you're on the bench you come to the conclusion at a certain time in the game that your chance of getting on the field is probably gone. Usually it's about the last 10 or so minutes when you feel you're not going to play. You concede the fact that you're not going to get on. I was thinking, 'Yeah sweet, I'll have to wait another week and see if I can get on the bench next week. I'm going to have to do that hard. I'm going to have to do the extras (when you don't get on for more than 20 minutes, you have to do the "extras" after the game).'

Suddenly, Roks (Joe Rokocoko) went down injured and I got the call. It was manager Tony Thorpe who said, 'Mils, you've got to get on.' I chucked my gear off and got out there as quickly as I could. I wanted to touch the ball as many times as possible. I was on for a grand total of about three minutes. England beat us 15–13. Dougie scored the only try of the game, but Jonny Wilkinson landed four penalty goals and a dropped goal for England. The disappointment of losing that game didn't really hit me until much later, since I was so over the moon to be an All Black. I probably didn't face the same pressures as the guys who during the week knew they were going to start. But no matter what else happened, at the after-match, I received my cap and I was an All Black.

The following week I got my first start. I was to be fullback against Wales in Hamilton. And that was an awesome feeling. Then I started again against France, and I slowly progressed to more regular selection. But the nervousness before the team is named has never changed, even after 70 tests. I'd have my phone ready when the team was being named. I totally forgot about the fact that they come and tell the guys who are not playing. I'd always tell Hayley before anyone else and I'd have my phone pre-set and ready to text. I'd have '15' or 'bench' ready in text, and then I'd wait. My phone would be on silent and I'd wait until the team was named. I'd go into the bathroom and I'd quickly send either 15, bench or DD (dirty-dirties or dirt trackers). I'd delete the ones that didn't apply, and push send.

Next I quickly jumped on the bus before everyone else got on. I didn't want to be the last on. I did that before all the games in 2003. Upon reflection it might have seemed a pretty dumb thing to do, but I was an All Black, and I liked being an All Black and you know that one day it's going to finish and it could be the next time. As it turned out, I wore No. 15 right through that 55–3 win over Wales, and the 31–23 win over France in Christchurch.

Once that part of the season was over Hayley and I decided to go to Queenstown and have a couple of days off. The Tri Nations squad was going to be named. I was still nervous about that. I felt I had played some good rugby but you're never quite sure whether you're going to make it or not. As it turned out, I made the Tri Nations team but Anton Oliver, Christian Cullen and Taine Randell didn't. I never quite understood why they missed out like that, and I was conscious that I might not be named again.

We had lost to England but in the rest of the games we played well. In the Tri Nations we thumped South Africa in Pretoria 52–16. There appeared to be wide open spaces all over the ground and Dougie and Roks scored two tries each. We came back to Sydney to play Australia and while there were some diverting issues about World Cup bonus payments hanging around, we beat Australia 50–21 — a record total and Roks went across for three more tries. The Springboks then came to New Zealand, to Dunedin where they had never won, and where they lost again 11–19, although that game is probably most remembered for the 50-metre run by Bok prop Richard Bands to score. The season culminated at Eden Park with a 21–17 win over Australia. Dougie scored twice and we regained the Bledisloe Cup for the first time since 1997.

Everything was going so well; it was all you ever wanted. It was more so for me after what I had gone through the year before and that year with my dramas. I had sacrificed drinking, had put everything into playing well, we had won the Super 12 and we had won the Tri Nations. Everything was great; the public were exceptional. And I really understood what it was to be an All Black. We were winning and, of course, that always helped.

I watched the naming of the World Cup team on television and I was in it again. From my point of view it felt like we had been successful all the way through and there were high hopes for a winning World Cup campaign in Australia. At the Cup things started well. I felt comfortable in the set-up and mostly started at fullback throughout the tournament. We were based in Melbourne. I had a great time, I was loving my rugby and I was really enjoying playing. A big plus at test level is that you only ever have to worry about your own position. You know that if you do your job, the other guy will do his. And if he wasn't doing his job someone else would come on. That was different from provincial rugby, even though you always talked about aiming for that level in the NPC.

What I really enjoyed about playing for the All Blacks was that you had to be clinical. You had to be up every game. You got limited opportunities, and you had to finish them. Apart from anything else, the sheer hype of being part of the All Blacks lifted you. Even things like getting on the bus and going to the games with a police escort had an effect. You drive past the crowds of people who were lined up at bars on the route, and see their reaction when they look up and see the All Blacks coming. It's an unbelievable feeling. They're cheering as loud as they can and you think, 'Far out!' It's like you're in a different world. I didn't want the excitement to stop.

I wanted to stamp my mark on world rugby and to play the game so well I would keep starting week in, week out. We were winning all our games. Looking back, I was a little naïve in my appreciation of the fact we were at the World Cup. One problem with being based in Melbourne was there was no real hype around the World Cup being staged. The newspapers and media coverage was much less than in Sydney and Brisbane and well below what you would see in other countries. We'd been so successful that I suppose in a little way we started to think we couldn't wait for the final. There was a self-belief, and probably some arrogance as well, that we were waiting for the final to arrive and then we'd really go at it. We'd won the Bledisloe Cup after we hadn't held it for so long, we'd won the Tri Nations, and next in line was the World Cup.

Things went smoothly through the initial stages. We opened with a 70–7 win over Italy in Melbourne and next played Canada there. I moved to the wing for that game and scored my first try for the All Blacks, in fact, my first four tries. We won 68–6. The other thing I remember about that game was that with Aaron Mauger injured, Dan Carter played at second five-eighths and kicked nine conversions — a sign of things to come. I moved back to fullback when we travelled to Brisbane to play Tonga. We beat them 91–7 and I picked up two more tries. We were given a bit of a shake-up by Wales in our last pool game and had to work hard before winning 53–37. It was back to Melbourne for our quarter-final against South Africa.

It didn't seem like there was any team apart from England, who we really wanted to play, that was going to come close to us. I believed we were going to win the World Cup. Once we made the quarter-finals we knew we could not take the Springboks lightly. However, we managed a comfortable enough 29–9 win over them. Before the semi-final against Australia we were probably a little bit ahead of ourselves and thinking more about the next game — the final.

We'd beaten the Aussies so convincingly two games in a row in the Tri Nations, and here we were again. We had the belief that we could do the job against Australia, but there were key moments in the game where we didn't finish. I knocked the ball on, when I should have scored a try. And the intercept pass! We were attacking in their 22-metre area for what seemed like an eternity. And we still couldn't score. Then, all of a sudden, they got the intercept. Before you knew it we were in trouble. There are certain instances in a game that make you think twice about things, and that's when we started to think twice. Mortlock scored that try and it lifted the Aussies. If we had scored, it might have been a different story. But that wasn't the case. We came back, but it wasn't enough, and that was it. Beaten by Australia 10–22.

The mental anguish of losing wasn't helped by the fact I broke a tooth in the game. So there was a physical scar that I had to face as well. Straight after the game I had to go to the bloody dentist who spent four or five hours removing and putting stuff into my mouth to try to save my tooth, but that didn't help my disbelief. The whole time I was wondering how the heck we could have lost, and I couldn't put my finger on it. I couldn't believe we weren't going to be playing the final the following week.

I went and stayed the night with my parents. When I got to their place I was very upset, and I had a decent bawl at their door. It was like a bad dream. I couldn't sleep. When I did, I slept about five minutes. I woke up staring at the ceiling. I couldn't accept that we'd been knocked out of the World Cup. It wasn't until my folks dropped me back to the hotel in the morning that I heard it on the news. Then it hit me, 'We're out!' There was your dream shattered. You always wanted to win that World Cup. Although I said I was a bit naïve about being there and how things had gone throughout the whole year, I still wanted to be taking the World Cup home. Just like the 1987 team had done.

It really hurt. I didn't realise how heavy the disappointment was until we came home. Everyone was going on about it; Mitch was given the gas. Perhaps it might have been different had I been in the team a bit longer. But that wasn't the case. It took me back to 1999 when the All Blacks were beaten in the semi-final by France. I was in Fiji on a rugby trip with Unitec and I couldn't believe then that we had lost. It's fair to say the 'frogs' where we were staying took a bit of a pasting that day. And I remembered how New Zealanders had reacted to that loss.

So I knew what people were going to be like about us missing out again. But before we got home we had to take part in the third and fourth play-off as well. And that is worse than anything. The whole week you sit there thinking what the heck you are doing there. It's a game that shouldn't even be played, to be honest. It's worth nothing. In it we beat France 40–13. We were up 14–6 at halftime. I scored a try in the second half as we romped away for the win. Once we got back to New Zealand I just sat at home for a few days and mulled it over. I still couldn't believe that we'd lost. I didn't watch the final. We did nothing for a month or so. But one thing was reinforced for me during that time. I did know I wanted to make the All Blacks again. I wanted to play some good rugby again. Obviously, with Ted being named coach, he was putting his team together and for players that can be a scary period, because you don't know where you figure in the scheme of things. I'd had Ted as a coach before but I still wasn't sure.

I did know that all the sacrifice and commitment I had shown the year before in order to make the team was going to have to be repeated, and it would have to be that way every year that I played. I had to try to make some more sacrifices that year. But it still hurts now, the fact that we lost that semi-final, and to this day I dearly believe we shouldn't have got ourselves in that position. And that's what they talk about: a test match is never a given. Perhaps the majority of the team thought that because the side had been so successful, the semi-final was going to be given to us. In fact every game is different, and it doesn't matter whether you've beaten them by 30 or 40-odd points the week before or whatever. You have to front the next week. The loss was a hard thing to take, but the fact is we had no other chance. We couldn't go out there and play it again.

As a 23 year old I wasn't as cut up about it as I was about the 2007 defeat, but it definitely hurt to come home and have to start all over again. The other thing was that I didn't know whether I was going to be hanging around for another four years. Four years seemed a long way ahead but I must admit it came round quickly.

With the benefit of hindsight and more time in the All Blacks, I think the team in 2003 was a lot different in its make-up. There were definitely cliques in the team. I was conscious that you always had to watch what you did and who you got on with and what you said to different guys. Other players felt the same way. Coach John Mitchell was good. I felt Mitch didn't come across on TV as the person I knew. He was a good guy and I got on with him really well. I had just got into the team and realised he had certain philosophies and different viewpoints on some things, but I respected that. Yet, in front of a camera he totally changed. I think if he had come across more like he really was then the New Zealand public would have liked him more. He was a genuine guy who wanted to be successful and who wanted the team to be successful.

As for Robbie Deans, I have to say I learnt a lot from him. You could understand why he made the Crusaders so successful. What he did with the backs was outstanding. The way the coaches wanted to play the game with width was one example. I never knew anything about 'width', about how wide you could play the game, until then. Playing the game with width was a big part of the Deans' approach. I couldn't believe that you could have the skill to get the ball out that fast, run those sorts of lines and get over that advantage line as easy as you could by playing a bit of width. Kicking had similar lessons and there was the need to have good body position when beating players. If we were going to go wide you had to make sure that you were nice and low so you were well placed for whoever came through at the breakdown.

We were playing a lot of sequences back then and it was a case of knowing who would do what. The flanker would go first, then the second five-eighths who might be taking the ball up, or possibly the No. 8. Then the guys that go round, No. 1, the closest lock, the farthest lock, and maybe the closest prop. I never knew that sort of stuff, I thought whoever was there would get the ball. It was like rugby back at school where whoever was there would run the ball here, or run the ball there. It was all so logical when it was broken down and it was a whole new part of the game for me. At the same time I was conscious that I didn't want to step out of line with Robbie, because I knew from stories I'd heard that if you weren't on his side then it was the highway. But I had no criticism of him. Both coaches were really good to me. At the same time I was in that sort of a fairyland where I knew that I was playing, I was starting. However, I still knew that one day that year I probably would be given the chop. When Leon was there.

Being dropped was a disappointment I always prepared myself for. I was always in a different frame of mind because of that. But until it arrived I was determined that I would keep playing as best I could. What I did know, when I look back at it now, was that a lot of guys were in there and had their own agendas. It wasn't as tight a team as what I imagined the All Blacks were. There was a lot of talking behind guys' backs about different things. I do believe that some guys didn't get in the team because they were spoken about to the coaches in a certain way that they were sort of disliked.

As a young guy coming into the team you thought that's just the way the All Blacks were, but the environment we have now is streets ahead. We learnt a lot from that period and I definitely believe the Canterbury guys learnt from that. Their attitude was a little like the Crusaders were so successful and to heck with everyone else, while those not from Canterbury were saying, 'Stuff the Crusaders.' Before 2004 you wouldn't even dare go into the group that went out with the likes of Reuben Thorne and Richie McCaw. And they probably wouldn't expect to have to come over to you and ask you to go with them. We've come a long way since then. That division alone created its own cliques. We've learnt a lot about not having cliques and getting to know different guys and what they do. Now we could go out for coffee with someone in the team from Canterbury, Waikato, Wellington, wherever, and that is as it should be.

But all the politics aside, I thoroughly enjoyed the experience of 2003, it was an awesome year. I know there was a lot of disappointment with the World Cup, but from a personal viewpoint it helped that I made the All Blacks for the first time. That really gave me an opportunity to stamp my mark on world rugby and it lit something in me to say I want a taste of this again and to keep being an All Black, year in, year out.

The 'yes' attitude

Things tend to move pretty quickly after World Cup failures in New Zealand rugby, but even I was surprised at the swiftness with which things happened after our 2003 World Cup ended. I couldn't believe that people were treated the way John Mitchell and Robbie Deans were. I knew we weren't successful, but the manner in which they were dropped was a surprise. I saw on the news that Mitch had been gassed without even being told. No person should be treated like that. Ironically, there was possibly a little bit of karma for him after the way he dropped the likes of Anton Oliver, Christian Cullen and Taine Randell at the start of his reign, something that I didn't agree with at the time. But, I guess it is true that unsuccessful coaches at World Cups don't really survive.

Apart from 2007. It was obvious though that something was going to happen after our semi-final loss to Australia, but I had never really taken any interest in how the process all worked. The way it all panned out was mind-boggling. A few weeks after the Cup, and after the interviews of coaches were done, it appeared that Mitch had been given the chop but hadn't been told. He turned up at Wellington Airport, I think it was, and there were reporters asking him how he felt. He didn't know a bar of what was going on; he thought he was going for a meeting. It made me wonder if it would be like that for the players as well. I didn't realise until later what wide differences there were between the NZRU and the two coaches. After hearing some of the stories later, I thought, maybe it was really time for both parties to part.

Even if the coaches are gone, however, the players are left, and because they are All Blacks they have to pick themselves up again and look to regain the winning habit. There were clearly faults that needed to be rectified after 2003 but the new panel of Graham Henry, Wayne Smith and Steve Hansen did not rush in. They had the home tests to play as their first assignment and they concentrated on making sure we got the World Cup out of our systems. England may have been the World Cup winner, but the side they sent out for two tests eight months later looked nothing like the World Cup side. Two big differences were that Martin Johnson, their inspirational leader, had retired and Jonny Wilkinson was injured. The All Blacks easily disposed of them 36–3 at Carisbrook. England fared a little better in the second test when the score was 36–12, but we played without Richie McCaw and Doug Howlett was also injured. I moved to Dougie's wing and Nick Evans came in at fullback. We got a taste of the rotational system that would become so infamous a few years later when 10 changes were made for our next test, a 41–7 win over Argentina in Hamilton.

Two weeks later we had a game against the Pacific Islands, a grouping of Tonga, Samoa and Fiji, and we won 41–26 at Albany. We made sure we held the Bledisloe Cup for another year when we won our first Tri Nations game, at Wellington, 16–7 in the pouring rain. And we had a home win over South Africa when Dougie scored in the corner in the last minute for a 23–21 win in Christchurch. However, we then lost to Australia 18–23 in Sydney and were hammered 26–40 by the Springboks in Johannesburg. We hadn't scored a bonus point in the entire competition and that proved costly as South Africa claimed the title that year.

That loss in South Africa was the turning point in the aftermath of the World Cup failure. I think the coaches knew they had to change things. The South African game was one we could have won. But the Springboks beat us up and won it really convincingly. We fell to pieces. We sat in the changing rooms after the game and everyone went round and said something about what they thought needed to change to make us better. I said that we needed to be a lot harder on each other and to be honest and up front with how we trained and to confront guys who didn't have the team's welfare at heart. I thought we weren't good at doing that. There were a couple of things that happened during the week that angered me.

We were still in that boozy mentality I suppose after 2003. A couple of senior players went out midweek and that surprised me. But what made it worse was that it wasn't a case of just going out and having a couple of drinks. They had a really big night and then came back and disturbed guys who were due to play, some of whom were starting. The way rugby was going we couldn't afford to have that sort of thing happen. Obviously it was dealt with by the management and we went on from that. It was out of that loss and the comments afterwards that the whole leadership group concept was created and I was fortunate to be part of it. We started having meetings every Sunday after Air New Zealand Cup games. We would go to Christchurch, or Auckland, and sit down and have a good chat about things.

Gilbert Enoka was working with us and we came together and slowly tried to establish how we were going to move ahead and improve. It wasn't so much the coaches saying it was going to be done their way. They wanted the players to be able to do that. We learned a lot of new things along the way. Initially, I remember thinking that after a game on a Saturday I couldn't really be bothered with doing all this travelling and meeting every weekend. But after a session you came away from it thinking, 'That was bloody awesome', and you realised you'd been in there for three or four hours.

It was a big turnaround for us, and there were a whole lot of things we came up with. There was no problem of acceptance of our decisions from the rest of the team because the leadership group was a core group of guys who were playing most of the time and who were well respected and whatever we said everyone accepted. The rest of the players not only believed it but they wanted to follow along. The leadership group was always conscious that we had to front and we had to be harder on those in the group than we were with the rest of the team. When the other guys saw the likes of Kevey giving it to Richie in front of them they knew that we were serious. Richie knew that he had done wrong and the fact that Kevey had given it to him suddenly opened up guys' eyes. It let them know that we were honing in on everything. We didn't accept things like dropped passes. We established something for the special jersey that we represented.

Gilbert played a big part in that. He was really good. I've heard a lot of people calling him Gilbert Echoker, or something like that. But he's a massive influence. If you had someone like that in your business and he helped you go through things in the way we had to go through, I think you'd be successful. It is a fact that after you go through something as major as a World Cup disappointment you can't just roll on up next time around and expect to take up from where you left off. We worked on our vulnerable points and exposed ourselves to other people's thoughts on us. And I think that's what made the team grow. There's something about seeing someone like Tana Umaga, who was putting himself out there in front of all of us, being vulnerable.

We were sent as a team to the Heritage in Auckland. We had one-on-one sessions, we had peer assessments. We had activities where two of the guys were up in front of us. They were given a sheet of paper and they had to write down three things that they were good at, three things that they thought they needed to work on, and so on. Then they went out of the room. The rest of us would form four groups — two would report on one of the guys and two on the other. It was just pure brutal honesty. There was no laughter. You had to look the guy in the eye. Richie and Tana went first. Obviously their reports were going to be pretty good because they were excellent players and good guys. But then as you kept going through the list you were hoping that Gilbert wasn't going to come and talk to you and say, 'Hey, are you ready?' You never had to participate until you were ready.

I had my assessment in Durban; I was one of the last ones to do it. It went on like that for a couple of years. It was tough. It's natural to write modestly and to write how you think people see you. I can't remember too many details about my assessment, but I do recall that it wasn't too bad. One comment was that I was too nice and that while I was seen as a really good guy I needed to tell it how it was sometimes. And that was something I found hard to do. But as a criticism of me, it wasn't bad. What was good about it was that I didn't really realise some of those traits that I did or didn't have. But by being purely honest with one another these things were pointed out. Before you knew it, it was starting to happen on the training field. Then on the rugby field it was there, and I know now that guys would still go out there to this day and put their bodies on the line, or they'd do their homework purely for the fear that they didn't want to let their mate down. That's why it's such a good environment.

Unfortunately, we didn't win the game that really counted in Cardiff in 2007. However, that didn't make all the work we had done pointless. Up until then, and even now, we're a bloody good team and have been really successful with what we've achieved in the last few years. And that's the result of the coaching staff knowing all that sort of stuff, including Gilbert and others.

The changes we made didn't have an immediate effect, as 2004 wasn't a very good year until our end-of-year tour. We talked about different things and how we were going to improve. I suppose that core, that leadership group, learnt a lot about how things are worked out. We had to deal with the fact that there were a lot of times where everyone was thinking about themselves, me, me, me. I remember we came out of that thinking, 'Hey, there are parts of us that just bloody want to succeed for ourselves', and it wasn't all about the team. We needed to look at ourselves, to have a 'yes' attitude with signing stuff, a 'yes' attitude with sponsors.

So we came up with the notion that it should always be about the 'yes' attitude. All Blacks do get swamped by a lot of demands, 'Can you do this? Can you do that?' You're often asked for autographs, or to have photos taken. And there are media requests. But we adopted the 'yes' attitude. Darren Shand, the manager, would say we had certain duties to do that day when we didn't really feel like it. Then someone would say 'yes attitude'. It got to the point where we'd all laugh about it, but actually, we were doing it without even noticing it.

We had to be open and honest at these leadership and team meetings and there were times when you didn't all agree. So we learnt to disagree and commit ourselves. Although you might disagree you still had to commit to the cause, as opposed to disagreeing and doing everything possible to bring the other guys around to what you wanted. I talked about the reconditioning window. A few of us disagreed about not playing in the Super 14 before the 2007 World Cup but we committed to the cause. It wasn't only things like that. It was how the week before a test was going to pan out, whether we were going to get a day off or not; all sorts of different things. We had sessions on just about everything and we really went back to the core about the jersey and what it meant. We realised that our time was special and that you create your own legacy in the jersey. Although the people in the jersey change, the jersey, its blackness and the silver fern never do.

It was our job to enhance the legacy and we wanted to leave a legacy of our own. We went back and learnt about the haka and it was from that that we got someone in to help us with an alternative haka. All of those things drew us into the fact that we love the All Blacks' jersey. And we love this jersey so much that we want it to bloody succeed and we'll do anything possible to succeed. All the young fellows who have come into the team have embraced that concept. And they're welcomed into the team now. Previously, I don't think they were welcomed as much. Certainly when I was first selected it wasn't the way we do it now. Now they welcome you in and joke and laugh about it. It's similar to what the New Zealand Sevens team does. You show the new players the ropes and you tell them what they need to know. Before it was never like that. You just had to find your own way.

When the new guys come in now they always thank the senior players:

'It's just been awesome the way you guys have helped me' and stuff like that. And that is the way it should be. There's nothing to be gained from being 'macho' and saying, 'You're playing in my position so I'm not going to talk to you' or 'You'd better pull your weight because you're an All Black now'. That might have been acceptable once but times have changed. The rugby player has changed and the mentality of players has changed. We're getting paid to do what we do. They weren't back then. There's none of the attitude of doing everything possible to make a new guy look like a dickhead.

It wasn't just the players who were involved in the changes we made. A few of the management also did the peer assessments. And we all had to live by it. I am convinced that, from 2004 on, the changes we made were one of the main reasons why we were so successful. That is, up until the 2007 World Cup, because we lived by all this stuff and we believed it and everyone wanted to be in the All Blacks to be part of this very special team. What it also does is speed up the process when you come together for games. You gel quickly. Previously, it would take you a while to get going and before you knew it you were playing a test match when you were only starting to know each other. After the game you would start to click and have something to talk about with one another. Now, it's just automatic. It's like you've never left the bus. Although you've been in different sides in the Super 14, you jump in that All Black bus, certainly for an older guy like myself, and it feels like you've never left. Everything comes back to you, it starts straight away. There may be a few new guys who need to be upskilled on how things work and what you can and can't do.

We went right back to knowing that you had to respect people. You had to pick up after yourself. That the bus had to be cleaned every time you got off, when you're at a hotel your room was never to be left in a state. You have the 'yes attitude' to go up and say 'Gidday' to people at the hotels. You treat people as you would want to be treated. And man, we were blown away by how much they actually loved us when we did that at the different places we visited. In Rome, and France, people were amazed how we behaved. That showed us that our system was worthwhile because, when you're away, you're also an ambassador for your country.

And the All Blacks brand is so big overseas that people not only know the big names like the Jonah Lomus, Richie McCaws and Dan Carters, but they know the All Blacks. I don't think people in New Zealand realise how big the All Blacks' name is around the world. You really appreciate the good comments or the letters that get written about how the guys have acted. People couldn't believe that that's how All Blacks were. They were genuine guys, not someone up there on a pedestal and untouchable. We respected people a lot more, respected the jersey more, and we acted like we were All Blacks 24/7, no matter whether you were in the All Blacks environment or if you had gone home. And that's the attitude we took and lived by.

When you come back into that environment, you love seeing your mates, you know that everything is going to roll on again, and you're excited about the challenge ahead. And you know that the guy beside you is going to go to war for you and will put his body on the line for you, because you're bloody good mates. You know that if you're not pulling your weight, he's going to tell you. You're not going to hold a grudge against him because you know that he's saying it purely for the fact that he cares about you and the team.

Perhaps we went away from that a little bit around 2003. It's different to the environment that you would have in Super 14 or Air New Zealand

Cup sides. I suppose it's a higher level that you know you have to perform at anyway. At the Chiefs we tried something similar with a group who work with the cricketers, Leading Teams, a different group to what the All Blacks worked with. And there was supposed to be no laughter. But when Wax (Sione Lauaki) was being peer assessed along with Sitiveni Sivivatu, he was asked, 'What do you think about him, Siti?' And Siti said, 'Oh, I don't really give a shit.' And everyone just started cracking up. The way Siti talks you laugh anyway. And he was then asked, 'What do you think about Wax's drinking?' And Siti said, 'Oh, to be honest I don't really give a shit.' Everyone started laughing again, including the facilitator. But that stuff had no meaning. Unless you're really committed to something like that there's no use doing it.

In the All Blacks environment we were dedicated to the process. People do go on about there being so many staff to support such initiatives, and, yeah, there may have been a couple too many, but the average punter doesn't know what goes on or the logistics of what the manager has to do, or the media guy. The PA has to sort out stuff and the baggage guy is there so the manager doesn't have to do it. Skills coach Mick Byrne has his kicking role, and then you have scrum coach Mike Cron. It's not that many when you think about it. I think the way they've done it, by having specific areas of responsibility is great. Backs coach Wayne Smith has the attack, Ted concentrates on defence, forwards coach Steve Hansen has the set piece and Mike Cron takes care of scrums. They're solely focused on one area. And they give each other feedback on different aspects.

Isn't that what you want? Don't you want guys to focus on one element and not worry about all sorts of other things? What they do is bloody awesome and they're world-class at what they do. What more would you want? You go into the All Blacks environment knowing that you're getting coached by the best guys in the world. Coaches who other countries would be prepared to pay a king's ransom for. And believe me, that is a pretty special feeling.

As a player who was increasingly being seen as a regular in the team, 2004 was important to my development and my understanding of my on-field role. I invited a mate to one of our games in Wellington a couple of years ago and he said he couldn't believe how much width we played the game with. The wings were standing on the sideline when we were on attack, and the fullback was round about the 5-metre to 15-metre lines. So stretching the defence and making them think how wide you are really stresses opponents. And if we get the ball out fast, we're really getting ourselves past the defence, who generally like to be pretty tight. If they are really tight, you're already over the advantage line by the time it gets out that wide.

It took a while to absorb that message. I first became aware of it when Doug Howlett or Carlos Spencer would come back to the Blues, or Auckland, from being away with the All Blacks and they would insist that we did things a certain way — the way they had been playing with the All Blacks. I guess that has been one of the strengths of All Blacks rugby through the years, the way these guys come back and pass on their knowledge and experience. I never got that kind of information from the Blues or Auckland coaches. One of the All Blacks would say to me, 'You've got to be a bit wider when we cut and when you cut someone, you've got to go back out, not cut in and go back into the traffic.' It's those things that make all the difference in the long run. Who would have thought that when you're supporting someone you've got to have a positive supporting line?

I never knew any of that stuff. And then to learn all that in one year, it almost felt like I'd just started rugby. I loved it and I wanted to try everything out and to know a lot more about this part of the game. There were all sorts of things. The way we played anaerobic games, the likes of touch. It gets your skills up. You're working at a level where you're stuffed but you have to keep going. Almost like sevens. And the little things you picked up while doing that were amazing. I never knew much about trying to get the right side up at the scrum; I was just the winger or fullback. I didn't know you had to get the right side up so you could attack down a certain channel and then if you attacked down a certain channel something else would open up. I was more like a robot: just do this, do that.

Once you learnt from different guys you could understand why Doug was scoring so many tries, or you understood why Carlos was making so many breaks at certain times. Or why someone was getting over the advantage line and getting there before you when you thought you had worked harder than him. What was happening was that he was actually being smarter than you. When you see that sort of thing at provincial level from All Blacks you thought it was just because of their greater ability. But when I made the All Blacks I discovered there were certain things in the game I could do to make myself better. That really excited me.

Previously, I had thought as long as I did my job that was all that I was happy about. I suppose it's more important to have all that information when you're first five-eighths so that you know who's going to come round. That's why those guys have so much influence in the way the team things are run. But for me as a wing and a fullback at provincial level it was a revelation. I was worried about getting my part of the game right. If Carlos created something, I had to be quickly into position to run off him.

I think the difference between the All Blacks and provincial rugby is that when you come to the All Blacks you've done all your hard work. You've done the pre-season training for Super 14, you've been figuring out how you're going to play as a team and what sort of game you are going to play. You still put in the work in the gym. But when you get to the All Blacks you've got limited time and you can't do any of that fitness work. It is all preparation. So, the whole week all you're doing is working out how you're going to play the game, why you're doing certain things, and then you go out and practise it. You're not doing the shuttles and there's not so much emphasis on weights, which were optional rather than compulsory at the lower levels. With the All Blacks it's solely about getting yourself right for that week and making sure that you perform that week.

As All Blacks we know how much pressure we're under. We can't afford to get things wrong. You can't afford it because you've got four million people who are after your bloody head. I'm used to it now, but I notice it when new guys come into the team, they're just amazed by the fact that all the focus is on preparation. It's all about doing your homework. You've got to get behind the computer, you've got to make sure you've got your book there, like you would at school, and you write all your notes down and go away after training and make sure you go over your notes again, so that when you come to training the next day you know what you're doing. If you don't put the work in, you get left behind. Everyone has got to be on the same wavelength, know their roles and know their jobs.

I had it rammed home to me. I went into my first year in 2003 thinking it was just the same as Super 12, but it wasn't. You had to make sure you had ticked all the boxes so that you were right on your game.

I appreciated the worth of preparation as early as the 2003 World Cup. Dougie and I were the top try scorers at the tournament, but there was a reason for that. It helped that I scored four tries when playing on the wing against Canada. But watching Dougie in action from a wing's perspective had opened my eyes to how he was scoring so many tries. The off-the-ball running that you do to create something with someone else has a key impact. All of a sudden you find yourself right in the support line. At one stage Ma'a Nonu was running the ball up and I was doing my off-ball running when, quick as a flash, he broke. I was the first person in support, and all he needed to do was draw and pass and he did that. Before I knew it I was over the goal-line. It really started to hit me at the World Cup. I went home and thought that if I did all this then I could be in the same sort of places in future. Some of it does rely on a bit of luck in that you don't get caught up somewhere. But for the majority of the time, if you're in the right place at the right time it's not by coincidence. You anticipate what's going to happen and you run the right line to be able to get there first.

Another positive development of the All Blacks has been exploring something of our understanding of our New Zealandness. I think New Zealanders in general tend to connect better with the emotional side of things. We really get wound up about some things and want to prove people wrong or to get even with someone who, in our case, might have beaten us. By the time of the end-of-year tour in 2004 there were many factors of our Kiwi identity and attitude that we really wanted to touch on. When we went to France for the Dave Gallaher Cup test we learnt a lot more about the First World War. We were quite taken aback by the sacrifices New Zealanders made in that conflict. New Zealanders were loved for what they did back then. We touched on that and then we looked at the World Cup in 1999 when the French beat the All Blacks in the semi-final.

Someone had got hold of a videotape which showed the French, after the game, doing a haka, and it looked like they were mocking it. I remember the team room that day after that tape was shown. The guys were teary-eyed. I think it was because they were so wound up about what we had learnt of those New Zealanders who were not much older than us who fought in the First World War, and then we saw that French haka and what they seemed to be doing. It was on the Thursday before the test and was all very emotional. When the guys walked out of that room they were ready to put fists through walls. They were so determined to go out there and do it.

Add to that a lecture we had had back in New Zealand before the tour about the haka and what it meant to us, and we were primed. Before that, none of us really knew exactly what the haka meant. To us it was just about being an All Black and because of that you performed the haka. We didn't appreciate that the haka is a piece of New Zealand. When we went overseas there was a something of New Zealand that we were taking with us and we were representing all our ancestors who had been in New Zealand for however long might be the case. We were made aware of that concept and that made it really special. It wasn't just the haka itself any more; the haka was part of our history and part of ourselves and we were showing that to the world when we were away. And we felt a connection with those First World War soldiers who were similar in age to us.

We were really pumped up for that game; we wanted to stick it to them. It started right from the haka that day. It was probably the most passionate haka we had ever done, and the rest spoke for itself. We gave them an absolute hiding in winning 45–6. We went away from that game thinking that we certainly left our mark on the French, and on world rugby. It was a timely win because it reflected the emotion of that build-up as well as the work we had been doing in our leadership group. It was a vast improvement on how we had played in the Tri Nations, and it set the trend for how we were going to play in the future. The first signs emerged when we played the opening game of the tour in Italy, and we gradually progressed from there. We beat Italy 59–10 after being up 35–3 at halftime.

We had a close call in our next game against Wales when winning 26–25. But I felt that game defined us as a team. We were a pretty young squad at that stage and to play a fired-up Welsh side and come away with a one-point win gave us a sense of belief that was borne out the following week. Wales led 14–13 at halftime and then scored first after the break. But almost straight after that I managed to score a try in reply, then Joe Rokocoko scored another to get us home by the point. It was Richie's first game as captain and there were a lot of us young guys in the side. What I found was that the guys in the leadership group who played that game, including me, had to put our hands up as leaders.

We were probably seen by most people as an under-strength team. We were just starting to get into that rotational mode, which meant we had to stand up as leaders and make sure that guys would follow us. Richie always said that you had to be better than your opponent if you were going to beat him. That was his attitude, and that was the mentality he wanted his leaders to have. It was a case of when you went out onto the field you had to play better than the opposition, whoever they were.

I wasn't a natural speaker or one who voiced my opinions but that was the start of me trying to put my hand up, more so with my actions than anything else. It also helped that I knew that I had the backing of management. When they had said I was in the leadership group I had wondered why the heck they had picked me. I didn't know what I was doing there, but it appeared that they felt what I said after the South Africa test had been a factor. I couldn't let them down and go out there and just become another player. I had to try to help the younger guys improve. I was determined to be a better All Black.

At one of those leadership group meetings Ted said he felt that I had plateaued. I thought his comments were pretty harsh, but I went away from that and wanted to prove to him that I didn't rest on my laurels. I wanted to have a decent tour. And that Welsh test was my chance to do it in a game where there was hardly any of us so-called senior players out there. It was a game the Welsh thought they should have won, and they definitely could have won. But we ground it out and although we won by only one point it felt like we had won by more than that, not because of the way we played, but because we had won a game that we shouldn't have won. It was a great way to lead into the following week in France because the mood around the team was of belief that we could actually do this.

The thing about the French game was that sometimes you can overdo the emotional side of things, but there are other times when we probably don't call on it enough. It was definitely a useful weapon when we played the French that day. We hadn't gone too well that year: we'd lost the Tri Nations and just managed to hold onto the Bledisloe Cup. We needed to have a decent tour and we came away successful and it started something special which we carried on for a few years. We knew we had the French when they put the white flag up and resorted to Golden Oldies scrums. The French are pretty hard men and can be passionate themselves. At one stage they were trying to suss out who was going to come on for a scrum, and there was actually someone who could play in the front row but then he decided he couldn't and we got a sniff then that they had done their dash. It was pretty early on in the game too. We got the sense that we were starting to get all over them and we were physically a lot better. We were very determined, and were ready to cut people in half. Our forwards showed the way that night.

Professionalism

Early in my career I thought I'd probably end up playing centre. And I've still got an ambitious thought that maybe as the years go on I'll end up there. But since I first started playing fullback, and as time has progressed and I made the All Blacks, fullback has been my number one preference. That's simply because I enjoyed it when I first came into it and that was the first position I played for the All Blacks. I enjoyed playing centre, don't get me wrong. The only thing was that I always felt that I needed more time there. A few times when I've been thrust in there it was a case of the team always coming first and it didn't really matter where I played.

Looking back I probably would love to have said this was going to be the position I'd like to concentrate on. But in saying that I think I've adapted well to the changes when they have been required. While it has been disruptive, at least you are getting a starting position and that's better than being on the bench, or not starting at all. It's only natural while you are striving to be the best in the world in one position, and you are played in another, that you get concerned. The likes of Leon MacDonald could have one great game and you might have a forgettable game at centre, and before you know it you're thrust into something else. That thought was always there. I'd never go out and have a game where I'd let myself down at centre, to reduce the chance of being played there again. But there were times when Leon was playing so well and the team needed someone to play centre, especially when we had just lost Tana Umaga, so you had to do it.

It was a bit better when we went back to provincial games. There was a time when I returned to Auckland, just before I was leaving to go to Waikato, and Brent Ward was playing so well at fullback that I was happy to play centre. I was at centre for the Air New Zealand semi and the final in 2005. Playing centre at the provincial level was all right because there wasn't as much heat to perform. You always felt comfortable at Super 14 level because it's a different sort of competition. Super 14 provides the opportunity for a lot of flair, whereas test-match footie has more pressure to perform.

You want to be at your best when you wear the black jersey; I certainly always wanted to be. But I always felt fullback was my position and the more I could play there the better I would get. I think 2008 was probably one of the better seasons I had in the All Black jersey. That was due in part to the fact that Leon was out with injury and because there were only young fullbacks coming through, I was able to concentrate there. The selectors told me fullback was where they saw me and that I was probably the fourth or fifth centre down the line. That suited me fine. But my attitude would have been the same if they had told me that they saw me at centre. In reality, however, at centre I always felt like I was filling in until someone had a decent game there. And then I'd go back to playing fullback. Had they said to me that they saw me at centre and to go away and make it mine, I definitely would have done that.

Every time I chopped and changed I always felt vulnerable to different aspects of that position. At centre my concern was in the contact situations, because at fullback you never actually train too much at being physical. Although you do make a few tackles, you never practise being really physical in the tackle. Then when I went back to fullback, I knew I had to be lighter despite the fact a couple of weeks earlier I'd been in the gym trying to get bigger. So when I got back to fullback I'd be puffing because I'd be running from side to side of the field, and then you went to centre again, where you're doing wee sharp bursts. And that hindered me a little.

At fullback I like to weigh in the low 90 kilo range. I could cope with 91–93 kilograms as long as my fat was low. There was a time when the selectors wanted me to beef up a bit and they told me to go away and eat as much as I could. I struggled with that. I'd have to eat five times a day, especially during the conditioning window, and I actually ate very well. It was porridge in the morning with some nuts, and by mid-afternoon I'd have a banana and a shake. I found all my portions got bigger and bigger until I couldn't eat it all. I'm usually not a big eater, but when I first started off it was a two-year process. It was the year before the conditioning window and the coaches said: 'You've just got to eat more, don't worry about your skin, your fat skin folds, just go for it.' So I did, and it didn't bother me at all.

My form probably dipped a little here and there but I was still happy. I had to be more demanding with myself in the gym. I've never particularly liked being in the gym, lifting more and more weights. But when it came to the conditioning window and the World Cup I didn't mind, as I knew

I had to get bigger. One part of me said it was going to be all right to play fullback at that weight, but I still had some doubt whether I could play comfortably with more muscle mass. I'd never done it before. I'm one of those guys who needs to prepare; I don't like going into something with my eyes closed. So to some extent I put on more weight and muscle, but in 2007 I probably did it the wrong year; I should really have done it a year earlier. I felt I reaped the rewards of that bulking work in 2008.

Another aspect to the physical development required by coaches is that you know what you are doing, and why. The coaches know, but the public don't. And if people perceive you are not playing as well as you should be, or that you look to be carrying more weight, they are not so understanding. It does help that the coaches are constantly in touch with you. But at the same time you are conscious that you don't want your form to slip, even though you are doing things at their request. While you want to hear that you're going to be part of their plans, you can't afford to tell yourself that in case your form does dip. I always got the impression from the way the selectors spoke that things would be all right. Once the All Blacks season came round, I was going to be there anyway, and things would start to improve. But it is harder to take on criticism when things aren't going so well, and you know that you're part of a bigger plan. You can't ring up a radio station and tell them what is going on.

The good thing about it is that you've got a coaching panel that you trust and it makes you feel easier. They tell you it's not going to happen now but it will happen down the track. In the last three or four years I have found I have gone through what was probably an average Super 14 and then all of a sudden the All Black season comes round and things start happening again. You don't really want to listen to the criticism and you don't really want to listen to who's coming through and who's playing well in the Super 14, but I think I've gone through sufficient years now to know that a couple of times there are guys who really come through and play exceptionally well. But equally you know that once the All Blacks season comes round and if some guys don't make it, all of a sudden there's another talking point. You just bottle up the criticism for three or so months and then you really let loose in the All Blacks environment.

I guess that at any time you can get dropped, and that's probably the scariest bit, even though you're not playing too well and the coaches are saying, 'Don't worry, this is what we're going to do here and here and here.' And despite the fact we have leadership meetings and you're part of that meeting every Sunday, there was still that element of 'Hey, I still might not get picked'. In those circumstances what I was thankful for was that although I had some pretty average Super 14 seasons where I knew I wasn't at my best, the coaches had faith in me to know that by the time I came to the All Blacks I'd be humming.

What is also difficult is the effect the needs of the All Blacks selectors can have on Super 14 coaches. You always want to play your best for your franchise, but you can't help wondering sometimes if the coaches are thinking, 'These guys are just waiting for the All Black season to start.' They want New Zealand to be successful, but they also want the Chiefs, or whatever team they have, to thrive as well. I think the All Blacks selectors do talk to them about what's going on and how things happen, and how guys are going. But I believe it's difficult for the Super 14 coaches to accept the fact that some guys are just not going to play at their best consistently in the Super 14 environment. There's no X factor.

The fact is that we play for so long we can't play at our best for six or eight months of the year. Guys come back tired and there are injuries that build up. I don't think people realise that it takes its toll on you. Most of us have days where we go to work when we don't want to be there and we sit at our desks waiting for the pay to roll on. Well, for us it's not so much the pay, it's the fact that it's the same old stuff again, 'Oh, we've got a meeting at 8 am, an analysis meeting at 8.30 am and then we've got a team meeting at 9.' And it just rolls on. 'And then we've got gym at 10.' A lot of it happens every day and you're constantly waiting for Saturday to turn up so you can go out there and play.

If you're going to do that throughout the year — I mean we started in January in 2007 with the pre-season stuff, right through to December, with a couple of breaks here and there — you've got to be superhuman to be able to be motivated to do that every day of the week. If you go right through to the All Blacks it takes a toll. And that's probably the difficult part for the Super 14 coaches to accept. Coach Ian Foster is very understanding. He won't make you come in until you're ready. And he won't make you be part of the planning process until you're ready. But it's got to be hard for them because they really want to succeed and the Chiefs haven't blossomed as much as they should. That's all part and parcel of professional sport around the world in many codes. From a player's point of view, if you want to go right through the whole season you've got to pick your moments to be at your best.

The public want you to be at your peak every game and, to be honest, I would too if I was looking at a rugby player. I'd say, 'Man, what do these guys do? They're supposed to be performing week in, week out.' But people don't know what we do behind closed doors to get ourselves right and all the things that we are trying to get right. The little niggles, the sprained finger, broken finger or chipped bone in your hand. Guys go out and play with those problems and it hinders them, but they still go out and do it. I think that's what people struggle to understand. Players have form slumps and fans can't understand why, because these guys are getting paid so much and they're not performing this week. Then all of a sudden they do come right, so what's going on?

Like everyone, we go through a process where we get bored and we need extra motivation. We need a little something to get us up and get our bodies right and rid of injuries that we've been carrying so we won't be thinking about holding back to avoid aggravating existing injuries.

Jack Dempsey, the heavyweight boxing champion, once said, 'A champion is someone who gets up when he can't', and I can relate to that. If I wasn't a rugby player, and I was a fan watching, I'd probably be criticising what guys do and asking why they don't perform so well. But when you're in the environment, and you have been an All Black, you know what goes on. You know when to get your body right. There's a certain time when you want to be at your best, and you come to understand the way your body works. And then, of course, you hope you won't get one of those bad injuries that can keep you out for a long time.

As my career developed, studying the opposition became a much bigger factor in how I prepared for games. I like to scrutinise the way a first five-eighths kicks and what he likes to do in certain situations: how they come out of the 22, and what they do before they kick. Earlier, I never used to look at that much at all. I used to think: 'Go out there and things will happen.' Now I'm very particular about observing those things. For instance, you can look at how many steps a first five-eighths will take before he kicks, and which way he likes to kick, how he sets himself up and whether the opposition run off the back of scrums in certain situations. Having extra information makes you feel better when you're out the back. By being prepared, and knowing how players react to situations, you feel more comfortable and can concentrate on other aspects of the game, safe in the knowledge that you have put in the groundwork and have a high percentage chance of knowing what they will choose to do at any given time.

It is something you have to do as part of your own preparation. But I must say that when Mick Byrne came into the All Blacks coaching crew as kicking coach I got more of an idea about how to analyse opponents. He'd done a lot of the groundwork for me by preparing his video clips of how different guys kick. But there are no short cuts. A lot of time is consumed sitting down in front of the computer and studying your opposition. You have to wait until their team's been named and you sit there sometimes for half an hour to an hour at times. You're constantly checking on different situations to make you feel a bit easier about going out onto the field.

An example of how it works is if we had a game coming up with Jonny Wilkinson playing, I would go and look back at the games he had played and see all the different kicks that he used. So you look at who's kicked in their side and the effectiveness of the kicks and whether they go out or not. I'd look at all the games he played that whole year, and click on each game and go through all the kicks. And you soon find little patterns emerging.

Mick was really good about pinpointing things in the work he did. For instance, it's not only about punting the ball. Before 22-metre restarts, Wilkinson always used to look up into the sky and wherever he looked, that was where he was aiming the ball. So we knew that 90 per cent of the time whenever he looked, it was either going to be a short kick off or a long one, to the right side of the field or the left. When you know things like that, it gives you that first foot in the door as to what they're going to do. It might not always be the case, but 90 per cent of the time it is. And if it is something different, you are ready to cope with it. I've found that a lot of the northern hemisphere kickers are very similar. While kicking they look at different things, or they step across, twice across their body before they kick and things like that.

You can also find out things players don't like doing. Ireland first five-eighths Ronan O'Gara doesn't like kicking to his left. Knowing what someone does or doesn't like gives you the opportunity to anticipate what will happen. As a fullback, I'd paint it as if I was going to stay on the left-hand side and give him the option of that right-hand side. But as soon as the ball's on its way to him I'd go across to the right-hand side.

Mick also passes the knowledge gained on to others. For instance, he would tell Richie McCaw about O'Gara not liking to kick to the left so Richie could pressure him into discomfort and mistakes. I think if you had a look at the last few years that we've done it, the majority of the guys have put a lot of pressure on their opponents who are kicking because they know how they like to kick, and we have a head start on running into the areas that the kicks will end up, or are supposed to end up. That puts a lot of heat on our opponents, and makes my job a hell of a lot easier. So what Mick does is great.

It does get frustrating when you hear comments from the public rubbishing why we have skills coaches. Those people have no comprehension of how effective they are. It's all about being ahead of the opposition, and the All Blacks have shown how important these types of methods can be. A fan generally wouldn't realise we're putting pressure on some area two metres away to the right-hand side, because we know that Ronan O'Gara, or someone else, likes to run that way. When we get a charge-down and someone scores it can look spectacular, flukish and against the run of play, but more often than not it is part of a plan.

And when you get rewards like that, it's massive. We know in our team environment how good it is. But, unfortunately, some critics don't realise how good the likes of Mick and others are as coaches.

As a player in a tight test match you never want to be in two minds about what action to take. If you can anticipate what opponents are going to do, and where the ball might land, you have a big advantage. It's not only the individual preparation either. As a back three, you and the wings obviously talk about your plans throughout the week before the game. Invariably, you find they've seen different things to what you have seen.

It helps when you know that the ball kicked by your opponents is going to land in a certain area because more often than not you can get there and catch it. That can be disheartening for a lot of the kickers and their teams. When they see you catching it on the full and running it back, as opposed to them chasing a ball that is bobbling all over the place or which has bounced behind the player's head, it can be a let down. It seems like they are playing more than 15 men. The other side of the coin is that when you do take the ball cleanly, through correct anticipation, you have more time to decide what you are going to do after you've caught the ball.

The experts talk about players having so much time to do something and this is one of the reasons why. To some it can be a natural skill, but for others it is the result of effective observation and preparation. We don't know whether our opponents are doing as much intense preparation as we are, but we have noticed that the Irish, especially, seem to be working in a similar style to what we've done and they've changed the way they do things.

There is also the factor that we strike in the Super 14 or the Air New Zealand Cup when we have to play against our All Blacks team-mates. Picking what Dan Carter is going to do is one of the hardest jobs of the lot. He's exceptional. He really works hard on his game, he analyses games well and goes out and does different things all the time. But for one who looks so naturally gifted people would be surprised at how hard he works on his game. I saw him come into the All Blacks environment as a real youngster, and the way he's developed his game is why he is, I believe, the best first five ever, if you could hold him up that high.

It would be difficult for the opposition to analyse DC. I've tried doing it during the NPC and the Super 14. It's next to impossible to predict what he's going to do and he's not afraid to try something different; he's quite expressive. One time I made the mistake of thinking I had his kicking sussed. We were playing the Crusaders and he was in his own in-goal area and he went to kick the ball. But he saw our guys had anticipated the area he wanted to kick towards, so he switched and passed the ball. For someone to do that, behind their own posts, is pretty freaky stuff. And they ended up getting 30 or 40 metres out of that. That's why DC's so good. He's not afraid to try things when the heat is on. And he studies the game so well. It's great to have someone like him on your side, that's for sure.

Matt Giteau is another who is always pretty hard to work out. Another Australian, Stephen Larkham, was similar earlier on in his career. He was so talented. He had a lot of flair and he could run the ball as well as kick it. Those two are the others who have been hardest to cope with, and Giteau is getting better and better. What makes them dangerous, and this is no disrespect to other players, is that I think they're more of a threat when kicks aren't on. They can run, and they are just as lethal with the ball in hand as they are when they're spiralling a kick over your head. That's probably why I'd say those guys are a lot harder to analyse, because they can create something when there's nothing really on.

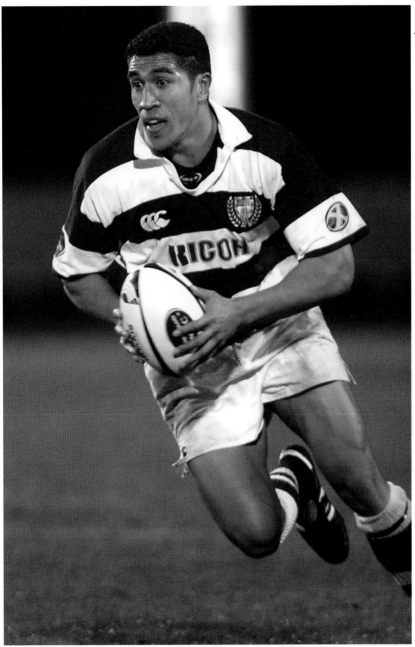

Fingers spread around the ball, eyes focused on the goal. Playing for Auckland against Bay of Plenty in Rotorua during the NPC in 2001.

Looking for support in the closely fought Super 12 final against the
Crusaders in 2003. We won 21–17.

Buried near the bottom right in the celebratory ruck for the photographers
after the 2003 Super 12 presentation ceremony.

I was only on Westpac Stadium for a few moments in my test debut, our 13–15 loss against England in 2003, but I wanted to touch the ball as often as I could.

Attempting to break around the Welsh defence in my first test appearance at fullback, at Waikato Stadium in 2003.

It's World Cup 2003 and I scored not only my first try for the All Blacks, but four of them, against Canada in Melbourne.

A great way to come back from the World Cup disappointment in 2003 was beating England at Carisbrook in our first test of 2004. Doug Howlett was in support and we enjoyed a 36–3 win.

The Bledisloe Cup was safe for another year after our 2004 success. Enjoying the moment with me were, from left, Mose Tuiali'i, Sam Tuitupou and Tana Umaga.

Above: We all wanted to share Tana Umaga's delight in scoring in the second test against the Lions in Wellington after his week from hell. From left, Rico Gear, Rodney So'oialo, me and Richie McCaw were all quick to congratulate our skipper.

Left: A special hug from coach Graham Henry after our whitewash of the Lions, completed with a 38–19 win at Eden Park in 2005.

The Springboks scrap every inch of the way in every test, and De Wet Barry was no exception when trying to stop me scoring at Carisbrook in 2005. But we won, 31–27.

A moment that meant so much to me — scoring in my last game for Auckland. It was the 2005 NPC final against Otago, which we won.

Australians are always tough to analyse. I've always put them up there in terms of respect because they're smart. They learn quickly and they also analyse the game well. I think they've got some guys who are really clued up. I've always been on my toes every time we play Australia, and you never want to lose to them because of the history we've always had. The other thing is that ability they have to learn from their mistakes, especially during games. They have the nous to be able to learn quickly from the different plays that have already happened. That's probably why they keep coming back and beating us in the last few minutes of games. They've always believed in themselves and they've learnt from mistakes during the game.

The Australian rivalry is an interesting one. That was seen in 2008 when the Deans-Henry saga was going on and everyone was wondering what was going to happen when the two countries met for the first time under the two coaches. That first game, in which we were given a 19–34 hiding in Sydney, was a funny situation because, despite getting done like that, and getting hammered by the media and public, there was a feeling of real frustration about the way we played. We were gutted about that. We actually played dumb rugby. We probably got too emotional and there were aspects of the game where we thought we were all over the Aussies and they weren't as good as what the score suggested. We knew we were a lot better than them. That belief and the out-and-out anger about the way we played was reflected in the way we played the following week back in Auckland at Eden Park where we not only beat them, we gave them an even bigger, 39–10, thrashing than they had given us. We were probably a lot more dominant in the breakdown and smarter in our tactics. The coaches were very good at that. I think that week was probably the calmest they've ever been, to be honest.

The senior guys had a meeting after Sydney and mentioned to the coaches that we needed a day off, and after a hiding like that when the week has already been scheduled, you don't usually get days off. For the coaches to agree to give us a break transmitted a level of reassurance that, hey, there was no alarm. They hadn't pressed the panic button. They were relaxed about it, as long as we had done our homework, and we'd had a pretty good week leading up to that.

Naturally, we were fired up about the way we played but we had the feeling that we were a lot better team than Australia and we could run the ball back and outplay them in that area, instead of kicking as much as we did in Sydney. The Aussies had just kept kicking back and we tired ourselves out in the end. We tried too hard to run the ball back and make the game faster. In the end they were playing smarter, by kicking the ball and having their forwards wait in between the 10-metre lines. They were getting a lot of rests and just setting up their defensive line. We turned our game around and did that in Auckland, and applied a lot more pressure on them. The coaches analysed where we could put the ball into space to be able to turn the ball over. We didn't send as many numbers into the breakdown as perhaps we did in Sydney, and we really hammered them.

I think that game was probably the crucial one in turning our season around. With the young guys we had, I thought that really stuck a big belief pill into the whole team environment. And the fact that we could be under so much pressure and still come away and beat a team so convincingly gave us a decent lesson about the competition not being as easy as perhaps we thought. We felt it was going to come down to doing the extra little things off the field, or studying our opposition to make sure that we were all on the same wavelength when we came to playing the game.

I know a lot of players say they don't read the newspapers or listen to the radio. And a lot of them don't, but sometimes you can't help but pick up the vibes. It doesn't help when guys are in the bus saying, 'Did you hear this? Did you hear that?' And then you find yourself asking, 'What? What happened?' And then you get all worked up about something stupid. You try not to get too wound up about certain things, but you do, and there's no way of hiding from it. On the bus we normally have music but one day no one had a CD and the news came on the radio and inevitably there was something about the game and how we would get thrashed. An announcer said we were going to get another hiding from Robbie Deans. So, you can't really escape, and it does give you extra motivation when things are down. That week was pretty tough, but we came through in the end, and definitely turned things around because we had put in the preparation. And that is the key to success in the professional era — preparation by all concerned in the camp.

The Lions' roar

No home season in recent times has produced as much excitement and anticipation as 2005 when the British and Irish Lions were to tour New Zealand. It wasn't only the public who got worked up about it, as players we also realised it was a once-in-a-lifetime opportunity to play against one of the legendary sides of rugby. It was 12 years since they had been in New Zealand, and after England's winning of the World Cup in 2003, all the elements were there for a memorable series. Even before the Super 12 season kicked off there was an amazing buzz around the whole country and you knew you wanted to be a part of it. I had a pretty disappointing Super 12 season and was a bit concerned about whether I would make the side.

I had personal problems that were publicised at the time and that occupied my mind a lot. I didn't produce any good rugby and that probably cost me a starting position for the first Lions test in Christchurch. By contrast, Leon MacDonald had played exceptionally well with the

Crusaders and he backed up again for New Zealand Maori when they beat the Lions in Hamilton. So I always felt that it would be touch and go whether I would start the game in Christchurch. The selectors had been very good about my situation. When you're not playing so well they keep in touch and try to work through any outside influences with you that might be affecting your game. Ted even invited me over to his place to chat about how everything was going.

I had quite a bit to do with Ted through those earlier years. He had been behind me when I joined the Auckland Academy at the start of my career and I had a bit to do with him when he came back to Auckland after being the Wales coach. He was a technical adviser for Auckland and then got involved with the Blues in 2003. I'll always remember after our winning the 2003 Super 12 when I had just been named in the All Blacks. We'd had our break-up and were on our way to a function near Northland and when we got there Ted sat down beside me and congratulated me on my season and said he thought I was going to be an All Black for a very long time. I chuckled at that, but he said he was serious.

I have always respected Ted for what he has achieved as a coach, but also for the way he relates to players. I always felt he cared about us. When he came on board in 2004 we started to establish the leadership group, of which I was a part. He was a different coach to what I had experienced before. He had an aura about him but you knew you could confide in him and tell him what was going on. Maybe that's just the headmasterly sort of way, but other coaches would ask if there was a problem. You'd say you were fine and they would leave it at that. But Ted's got a knack for knowing when you say things are all right and they are not. And if you don't tell him he can be persistent in finding out what the story is. It is not a direct approach, more in a quiet and courteous sort of way. He'll ring up, or when you see him he'll ask how things are and how the family is. I found it easier to be able to talk to him in that regard about what was going on in my life, especially since as All Blacks' coach he was very open and you obviously wanted to get on his side as well.

Another example occurred in 2002 when after my off-the-field incident I had addressed the issue and felt like my rugby was going nicely in an Auckland team that was playing very well and winning. I was happy with how things were, even if I had a feeling that my own contribution wasn't being recognised much. But at one practice Ted came up to me before the warm-up and said: 'Mate, I think you're playing some fantastic rugby and I want you to keep it up, it's awesome. I know that you're not getting the accolades in the media, but I definitely think that you're playing some fantastic footy.' From memory we had just beaten Canterbury when he came up and said that to me. I wasn't expecting anyone to say something like that. I knew I'd played well in the previous three or four weeks and perhaps it hadn't been highlighted as much. But for him to come up and recognise that left me feeling that he cared a lot about how I was playing and perhaps he felt that I needed a boost. If that was what he was thinking, it worked, because I felt I played even better afterwards as we won the competition. It was pretty exciting stuff.

It has been interesting working with Ted. It became obvious immediately how good a coach he was. The clarity he brought was most impressive. He was defence coach, but I don't think I'd ever had a coach so thorough in his debrief or as comprehensive in the way he made guys understand what they were doing. Ted made you aware why we were doing something and why we would lean that way. There were certain things he pointed out that the opposition did that we could probably stop at the source. An example was his observation that Australian halfback George Gregan always did an arc off the top ball in a lineout, and if you were at least a little bit wider you could cut that ball off and go a long way towards ensuring that Stephen Larkham did not get the front foot ball he wanted. It was good, detailed stuff, which makes all the difference. He would sit in the analysis room and go through all the clips he had and then announce to us, 'This is how we're going to go out and do this thing, this team, this opposition, and this move.' And then we'd go out and do it.

The selectors love it. They analyse everything about the opposition and all the scenarios. They may have seen that the opposition had five four-man lineouts, all between the 22-metre areas, and that there were certain moves they executed off them. That's how thorough they are. It may be that on the day the opposition don't use that particular tactic, but it means you are aware of some of their options and can work out what you need to do to stop them. It clarifies for you what you need to be watching for on the field. I found that intriguing.

Although it sounded sophisticated and technical, it was simple in the way Ted did it. He must have spent hours analysing. To this day he still does it, because every time you walk past his room he's sitting in front of the screen writing notes and putting up sheets of paper. He almost seems a little possessed by it, but he is certainly thorough.

They say rugby's a simple game, and it is, but you've got to make it simple by doing your homework. As a player there is nothing better than knowing what teams consistently do, say, when coming out of their 22, or what they do off a left-hand scrum or a right-hand scrum, or where their wing stands. You're a lot more comfortable thinking about what they're most likely to do. Yes, there is always the element of the unexpected and the fact that opponents will obviously be analysing the way you defend as well. But most of the time if the analysis is that clear you think that you've got most of the options sorted. It's a good mindset to be in.

All the All Blacks coaches do a hell of a lot of work. Smithy is just like Ted in the way he analyses the game. We're always saying to him to take time off and get away from the laptop. They are that passionate and I suppose they feel that if they don't keep at it often enough, they may feel uneasy about it. The feeling they give is: 'Will the opposition be taking a break from their computers? Can we afford to do less than them?' But there is no doubt from a player's perspective that the effort they put in makes our job a hell of a lot easier. You just go out there and concentrate on playing rugby.

For all the disappointments I had with the Super 12, I recall going down to Christchurch very excited about the Lions. I was raring to go. I was carrying an injury, having hurt my shoulder in the second last game for the Blues, which was my 49th game. So I missed the last game in Sydney and never got to play my 50th game for the side. My shoulder was a bit inflamed and I was receiving injections to try to bring it down. I was a bit uneasy when I went down to Christchurch, mainly because you don't know whether you are going to be named in the side. You hope that the coaches aren't going to come looking for you in the changing rooms, or at your room at the hotel. I suppose I was more on edge this time because I'd had such a disappointing Super 12.

Ted came up to me in the changing rooms just before we ran out to train on QE II Park, and he said, 'Listen mate, you're on the bench.' And I suppose you sort of stop for a second when you hear that. You see him coming and you hope that because they've left it that long perhaps you are going to start. He obviously hadn't been able to find me; I was clearly doing a good job of avoiding him. But he said to me, 'We really need you to be up this week.' And, of course, I said, 'That's awesome, that's great.' You are disappointed but you realise you're still in the 22. It was the Lions and you wanted to be part of it. I had to put on a brave face, and go out there and train. That's probably the hardest thing when you don't get named. You have to carry on and forget the fact that you're not playing.

I went out and saw Leon MacDonald and said, 'Well done mate', as we were warming up, and shook his hand. Steve Hansen came up to me and said, 'We need you up this week', so they knew how I was feeling. Or perhaps he was just doing it to all the guys. But you get over the disappointment, after the warm-up and the first grid. As the days progress you just want to be there to help out the starting XV. And that's your sole role, to keep them honest and hold the shields and also give feedback.

We believed it was going to be a close series and every game would be hard. The fact that the Poms had won the 2003 World Cup and the pendulum of world rugby had dipped slightly towards the northern hemisphere added to the pressure. The hype of it all, and the Barmy Army getting involved, meant it was going to be a great series and we were definitely looking forward to it. But we couldn't get a gauge on how hard it was going to be or how good they were, because they never really played their test side in any of the warm-up games. And then the New Zealand Maori beat them as well, which could have made them even more determined to come out and give a really good performance. There was no way that we had thought it would turn out like it did. The weather played a big part in Christchurch, and we played some outstanding rugby in the conditions to win 21–3. Our forwards took it to them and our backs played some classy stuff in testing conditions. It hailed at one stage, which was probably the one time you're actually quite glad you're on a bench because we kept ourselves pretty warm that evening.

The atmosphere was outstanding, and I think you can probably soak it up a bit more when you are on the bench. When you're playing you don't tend to look at the crowd; you've got too much else to be watching out for. I found it was a phenomenal experience and was grateful to be part of it. Although I only got a couple of minutes on the paddock, because Leon's hands were frozen, it was still another test match, and I wanted to get out there and play the Lions. You think you may never have the chance in your career to play them again, and I don't think I ever will. So, it was a great experience.

The big thing that came out of that first test was the incident when Lions captain Brian O'Driscoll dislocated his shoulder after being spear-tackled by Tana Umaga and Keven Mealamu. That incident loomed over the lead-up to the second test, more so because of the way the Lions were complaining about it in the media. Our guys were a little annoyed about the whole incident and the amount of coverage it was receiving. Given the fact we'd played so well and outclassed them right across the park, all the attention was focused on O'Driscoll, and how we had dislocated his shoulder. I lost a little bit of respect for him as a player in the way that he handled himself. I'm probably biased because of the way that I regard Tana and Keven. I had always thought highly of O'Driscoll. During the Grand Slam tour later that year I saw him at a pub, and he said how sorry he was about how things worked out and what happened wasn't really him. However, rugby players don't usually come out and whinge the way it seemed he had at the time. I suppose looking back he might have had a case to be able to complain, but I just didn't like the way it was all handled. And given the fact it was one of your mates who was involved as well, it wasn't very pleasant. With the Barmy Army and the legion of other Lions fans about, the boys got a lot of stick that week and it was a testing time for both players. More so for Tana, I think. To come back and play the way we did, and the way that Tana played, was great.

Whether Tana should have gone over and shown some concern when O'Driscoll was going off is only a question Tana could answer. But I think when you look at the incident, and it does look pretty rough, sometimes you don't realise what a player's done and why he's gone off and how severe his injury is until later on. If you were on the other side it is understandable that you would feel Brian did have a case and was right to be annoyed about what had happened and how it occurred. But the whole hype surrounding the Lions' management's reaction got to our players. The series itself was definitely far more intense in pressure and excitement than anyone had anticipated.

The week before the second test was a disrupted one, but we just wanted to get that game under way and go out there and be really physical and take it to them again. Their coach, Clive Woodward, had been outstanding with what he had achieved with England. Yet before the 2003 World Cup he had been about to get axed. To come back from that and coach a team to win the Rugby World Cup — you have to have a bit of respect for the guy. But I know his reaction to the spear-tackle incident annoyed a lot of the players. We were determined to make sure that by the time the second test finished everyone was talking instead about the way the All Blacks played.

I started at fullback in the second test in Wellington. The physicality in the first few minutes was second to none. The Lions came out fizzing just as we had expected. They'd got rolled that first week and they were ready to make amends. Gareth Thomas, their replacement captain, scored first. I remember him stepping inside Keve and there was just me left. I was probably a little bit too wide, given the fact that there was only 20 metres to go, and he scored under the posts. It was the perfect start they needed for that game, but the All Blacks showed a lot of composure.

There were four elements of our game that we were really big on, and one of them was the 'now-focus'. That meant that you had to forget everything that had happened and just focus on the next job at hand. Whatever was called you had to make sure you knew your role in that play and to focus on winning that next moment. I do recall a lot of that being said, 'Don't worry, now-focus boys, now-focus.' It was early in the game when an early try by the opposition can set you back a lot. We were seven points down but we steadied ourselves, went back and started again. Having those cornerstones in our game has helped us a lot, especially the 'now-focus', when things aren't going too well. It still gets said a lot because in the hype of the game everything's going a million miles an hour. You've still got to do the next job and it could be as simple as just catching the ball or making the next tackle being the now-focus.

It took us a while to get all our cornerstones in place on the end-of-year tour in 2004, but we carried them through to 2005. We felt if we could always achieve those few elements, we'd go a hell of a long way towards winning a test match every week. You almost felt uneasy if you didn't do things right, so it was a good element to have.

Of course, one person who did do things right in that game was Dan Carter. He was brilliant. Those tries he scored and the way he kicked meant his game raced up to another level and he stamped his name on world rugby as an outstanding player and as a superstar. Having watched him develop, you always felt there was something special there, but for him to bring it out against the Lions was unbelievable. They had all that experience, with players from four nations involved. I couldn't believe how he tore that team apart with sheer strength. He had to fend off the likes of Gavin Henson and go through and set Tana up for his try, and to then come back again and grubber through and have the ball bounce perfectly for him to score a try, and then sending the ball wide again and he backed up and was rewarded by scoring again, out wide. I remember all those tries because you sit back and wonder how the heck he managed to score them. We were definitely stoked about the 48–18 win. We'd taken it to them and we knew that Dan played a massive part in achieving the win. We all know now what he's gone on to achieve and how big he is in the game of rugby. Like everyone, we'll be watching to see how he recovers from his Achilles tendon injury.

Wellington was buzzing afterwards. Not only did we win, we had also ensured the series victory. We went to the after-match knowing we had done a good job and everyone was thrilled at the way it had panned out. But Monday soon came around and knowing that we wanted to make history with a clean sweep, we still had to win three games in three weeks. Although we had the series we wanted to play well and finish off on a good note. While you tell yourself you don't want to take the foot off the pedal, you're in that state where you ask yourself: 'Do I have the excitement to go out there again and make it happen, and make it happen so it's 3–0?'

There were a few changes in the squad as we headed to Auckland. Dan was injured so Luke McAlister came into first five-eighths, while Conrad Smith started at centre. And those changes might have helped us in a way. Sione Lauaki started at No. 8 with Rodney So'oialo and Jerry Collins on the sides of the scrum. Greg Somerville came onto the tighthead of the scrum for Carl Hayman. Those guys hadn't played much. And they were going to come out and really explode and get a piece of the Lions for themselves. Conrad, who scored a try, and Luke had big games. Tana scored twice and Ali Williams and Rico Gear scored one each in the 38–19 win. I recall after the game how proud we were at what we had achieved and how big a night we had. We just kept yelling to ourselves 'Three-nil, three-nil.' It seemed like that was your whole rugby career, that you'd done everything you wanted to do. Apart from the World Cup ...

The series win was outstanding and it was great for the country. When we went out to celebrate in Auckland I thought the Lions' supporters were absolutely brilliant. New Zealanders could really learn a lot from the way the Lions fans supported their team. Although they got beaten 0–3 they were still out there having a lot of fun. I suppose the pound's better value compared to the New Zealand dollar always helped, but I felt the way they came up and congratulated us, and were really humble about it, was great. They might have been disappointed, but they were good sports, still partied and had a lot of fun. To see them out enjoying themselves and not moping around or causing trouble, or abusing players, was great. It was almost as if they were supporting us, with the way they were carrying on. They were there to support the rugby, and they felt that the way we played the game was something worth celebrating. That is quite a contrast to most New Zealanders' attitudes. But, in saying that, I think we've come a long way from where we were. When you run into New Zealand fans overseas you know that among the first things they are going to say to you is 'You'd better win, you'd better win.' But when you are travelling you are stoked to see them because you're a long way from home and they've come a long way to see you and support you.

Down but not out

If I had any thoughts of euphoria after being a member of a team claiming a clean sweep over the British and Irish Lions and regaining the Tri Nations title, Auckland would soon provide me with a frustrating crash to earth. We had four weeks between the last Lions test and the Tri Nations starting, and we needed that time after the intensity of the Lions series. But it also meant we faced a tough opener against South Africa.

The Springboks gave us a reminder about the realities of international rugby. I was on the wing, with Rangi (Leon MacDonald) back at fullback, when we were beaten 22–16 at Newlands. In that match the Springboks got out to a 13–0 lead and while we pegged it back to 13–13, Percy Montgomery's boot got them back in the lead. We were forced into playing hasty catch-up rugby, and we made some uncharacteristic mistakes under pressure.

I was back to fullback a week later in Sydney when we were down 0–13 again before we managed to score 30 unanswered points to take a win. However, it was at the cost of losing Dan Carter to a broken leg. It was a victory which actually highlighted our failure to make the most of our chances.

The Springboks had to travel to Dunedin for the return game. It was late in the match before Kevey appeared out of a maul close to South Africa's line and scored the match-winner in our 31–27 victory. That meant the last game, against Australia, would be the competition decider and it was to be played at Eden Park. We were up 20–5 at halftime and we claimed a 34–24 win with Doug Howlett scoring three tries.

It would seem strange that, after all that success in 2005, I would regard the season as probably the worst year of my rugby career. Unbelievable as it may seem, I lost the passion of playing for Auckland. I loved Auckland rugby, I loved everything about it. I loved the fact that people thought Auckland was arrogant. I loved putting on the blue and white hoops. I never thought of playing for anyone other than Auckland and the Blues. My contract was up for renewal after three years. I had a meeting with David Nucifora and Joe Schmidt, looking at my options with the Blues, because I had received an offer way below what I knew was the market rate. I didn't want the moon; I just wanted the market rate. I couldn't believe the figure I was offered.

Chief executive David White went to the media with his comment that it was one of the most attractive offers he had ever given anyone. We went to the market and Waikato and Wellington came back with similar offers, a grand or two between them, both of which were streets ahead of what Auckland had offered. Wellington was offering slightly more, but I made the decision based on family reasons. So I signed with the Chiefs and Waikato while I was away with the All Blacks. I knew it was going to be a different experience, but I was looking forward to it and felt like a weight had been lifted off me. It was going to be like a freshener for me and I felt like I needed that. From 2000 I had been going through the same old things, the same old principles and philosophies. While I loved Auckland, a change was exciting and I couldn't wait. It was going to be a new chapter and I wanted to have a clean start and to play some good rugby without any baggage. But before I did that I had to finish my time with Auckland.

When I got back from the Tri Nations I had a phone call from Heath Mills, who was on the Players' Association. He said he wanted to catch up with me and see how I was. I had a coffee with him in Kingsland and got a feeling that the meeting wasn't about how I was getting on. I told Heath that I was keen and I wanted to make the campaign a really good one because I'd given seven years to the blue and white hoops and I was really passionate about Auckland rugby and wanted to have a real good go at it. From that meeting, though, I got the feeling he was trying to say that I wasn't excited and was enquiring how I would feel if I left my contract early. I was stunned! That's not the way I do things and there was no way that was going to happen. I was probably a little naïve. He then said: 'Oh well, shall we go talk to Pat, then?'

I agreed to that because I was intending to meet with Pat Lam to talk about all this stuff. So, we went to Eden Park and met with Pat. It was a whole different scenario from what I experienced the year before. After the 2004 Tri Nations I had gone back to training earlier than required with Auckland because I was keen to hit the ground running in the NPC. I wanted to know all the moves. In my end-of-year review Pat commended me for that because I was the only one of Auckland's All Blacks who had done that. But it was made clear to me that there would be no place in the Auckland team for me. I was in a quandary as I needed to keep playing rugby if I was to be selected for the end of year tour to Britain.

I left the meeting thinking there was no way I was going to be able to make that tour. Everything had been going so smoothly but I wasn't going to get the game time I needed. So, I rang Ted and said to him, 'Look mate, I don't think I'm going to get much game time, to be able to make the end of year tour. I've basically been told that I'm not going to make the team.' He said, 'Oh well, you just do what you've got to do, mate, and go out, and if you have to play Bs, that's fine.' I was very disappointed in the fact that I was going to possibly end my Auckland career playing for the Bs. Jeff Moon, the Bs coach, rang me straight away and said, 'Look, I've heard what's happened, we would be privileged to have you.' That was great because I thought for a wee while they weren't going to pick me for the Bs either. But to have Ted say what he did and then for Jeff to ring made things a lot easier.

Although I was very disappointed I knew it wasn't because of my form, and I felt at ease that at least I would be able to play some more rugby and hopefully be good enough to be selected for the tour. I don't know how things got round, but it would have been about five minutes later when my phone rang and it was Wynne Gray from the *New Zealand Herald*. I don't know how he got my number but he knew everything that had happened. I had just got back from my meeting and I don't know how it all came out. He said to me, 'So, you're not going to be playing in the team?' I was taken aback and, frankly, a little bit shell-shocked, and said I didn't know how things were going but at that stage I'd just play wherever they could fit me in. That was soon made public, which I didn't particularly need at the time.

However, I soon got over that and, in fact, I never played for the Bs because by the time things came round Auckland's injury worries meant I went down to Canterbury with the NPC team and I was on the bench when we played, and lost, to Canterbury in the Ranfurly Shield challenge, our last round-robin game. Pat had picked me on the bench, which I was pretty happy about, and then the following week I started at centre. In the semi-final against North Harbour, I was playing all right and there was a chance of starting the final against Otago and at least finishing my career with Auckland the way I really wanted to. And that was to play in a final and to play in the number one team. It was a pretty emotional week as I didn't really want to leave. Auckland had been so supportive of me as a youngster and to be leaving like that was tough. Anyway, when we won the final it was great. That finished it off perfectly for me.

It was hard to say goodbye to all my mates. I said that hopefully one day I would be back. The boys gave a bit of a cheer. I went down to Hamilton and got a great reception. The people were fantastic and I couldn't have asked for anything better in terms of support. Even before I left Auckland I would be in the street and people were coming up to me to say 'Go Waikato'. I didn't realise how many Waikato supporters there were in Auckland. For seven years it had been drummed into me to hate these guys from down State Highway One and here I was about to play for them, in what I thought were the ugliest bloody colours in the world.

With my decision made and the NPC completed I went back into camp again with the All Blacks and now the talk was all about a Grand Slam. We were also aware that it was 100 years since the All Blacks had first toured Britain and we were keen to acknowledge that fact. We also knew that only the 1978 team had ever achieved a Grand Slam and we wanted to make history again. We knew the northern hemisphere teams would be baying for our blood given the fact we'd beaten the Lions so convincingly. But we also wanted to go out there and stamp our mark on the year again. The big thing was that we wanted to leave a legacy of our time in the jersey. This was another opportunity to do that — to be part of a Grand Slam winning team. That would cap a great year. We were pumped and we couldn't wait to get on that plane and get over there to do the business.

Striking Wales first was massive. We'd narrowly beaten them the year before with a relatively inexperienced team. Richie had captained the team for the first time, I was part of that team that ran on, and we came through and won by one point. So we knew how loud it was going to be there, and how excited the Welsh team was going to be. We arrived about a week early and a few of the boys went out and got intoxicated, someone had taken their photo, and they quickly appeared on the front page of the newspaper holding the 'wrong' brands of beer bottles.

Once again, we didn't start the tour off that well. We hadn't even started playing rugby and controversy had erupted. There was a lot of soul-searching that week, because several of us were disappointed at what the guys had got up to. I was one of those who were disappointed. I was big on doing well on this tour and stamping the mark of the All Blacks on world rugby. By doing that we could demonstrate how far we had come since 2004. We had learned to voice our opinions and were able to tell our mates how we felt about their actions. Much of that week was centred on sorting it all out. It's difficult when you know it's one of your mates and it can be hard to tell them that you're pissed off about what they did. They made a wrong decision and a lot of us voiced the fact. It doesn't help that the incident was all over the news and back in New Zealand. Some of the players were finding it hard to try to explain to their wives why they were out and posing for innocent photos. I remember Tana getting up and saying, 'You guys who went out that night stay behind, the rest of you guys, out of the room.' There were guys who had only gone out for half an hour for a couple of drinks and then returned who stayed in that room. The leadership group laid it down hard that that wasn't the way we were supposed to prepare for a game and there were things said that really hit it home to those guys. I was pretty disappointed about it all and I voiced that in that meeting. So did a lot of the other guys.

It was great to be able to air it all, something that had become part of our team development. For a number of years we couldn't do that. We wanted to be the nice guys, on and off the field, and we didn't want to confront our mates. But doing this you were telling your mate how much you respected him, and they respected you in turn for that. So that was great. It was all done in front of their faces and not behind their backs. I think that cleared the air for everyone, including the offenders. They apologised for what they'd done, in front of the whole team, and that was it, done and dusted. We were back into training the next day. And those guys probably trained harder than anyone else. We were able to carry on with the tour and we got the ball rolling again. It was fantastic. Tana as a captain was pretty good at confrontation. He was big on that. I know that he went into the rooms of a couple of the guys and really gave it to them, because we still laugh about it today. They soon got the message that they weren't going to stuff up again.

So with all that behind us we went into the Welsh game and started the tour off well. Wales was the last place we needed to trip up, given the fact the 1905 game was where one of the greatest rivalries developed. The loss on that day, with the disallowed Bob Deans try, was the only test Dave Gallaher's men failed to win, denying them the chance of claiming a Grand Slam of their own. We kicked off our bid to achieve it with a convincing 41–3 win. We led 13–3 at halftime and finished with five tries, three to Rico Gear and two to Dan Carter, which were all converted by Dan. He added a couple of penalty goals and it was an outstanding way to finish off that week. And the guys who went out stood up and were among those who played well.

We were really humming and wanted to get onto the Irish test and keep going on our merry way. The difficult part was that the selectors started to rotate players. There was some nervousness about that because we wanted to win a Grand Slam and a complete change of teams was made for the test against Ireland. It was a huge risk but the selectors were confident we had the ability to cope. With all due respect to the Irish, the wholesale changes weren't because we thought they weren't any good or to show that we could put a team that everyone thought wasn't our best team out and still win. It was that the coaches knew from experience that we needed guys playing regularly all the time. I suppose that was the start of the rotating, as they called it. It was difficult for some of the players to take. But for the majority of the team it needed to be done. It was best for the team.

The coaches had the vision to say the players chosen would be excited about their chance and would go and play well. Meanwhile the guys who played against Wales would have the game off against Ireland and would be ready to go the following week against England. They backed their instincts and their coaching ability. I'm sure the coaches had no doubts the side would win, even when up against an Ireland team which had played very well in the Six Nations.

When we arrived in Ireland there was all the hype again about the O'Driscoll incident and Tana copped some abuse. He had to have some security when he did an Adidas visit. The public were lining up to get autographs and they said a few things to him, but he showed he was bigger than that. He didn't take that to heart and he just carried on his way. But it was always going to happen. Brian O'Driscoll is loved in Ireland and being the captain there was a fair bit of sympathy for him.

Despite the distractions, the guys who went out to play in that Irish game were probably the most prepared All Black team I had ever seen. They were building up for their game the whole week that the rest of us were preparing for Wales so they actually had two weeks of preparation. And that showed in the game and in the way they played. They went out and absolutely gave it to the Irish. Beating a good side 45–7 was pretty impressive. Jason Eaton and John Afoa made their debuts in that game. Richie captained the side for only the second time, while Nick Evans played first five-eighths. What their effort proved was that there was going to be stability in the way that we rotated, and that New Zealand rugby was looking pretty healthy so long as we could keep these players playing. There is always a lot of comment when the northern hemisphere teams bring second-string sides down to the southern hemisphere and they always go on about how the All Blacks have rotated in the past. But we have always taken our best players away, and rotated on that basis. There is also another significant difference — the All Blacks may have used rotation, but they kept on winning.

I think what the selectors have done is that they have tried to get a lot more guys experienced in playing more test footy. It's pretty hard and they cop a lot of flak again, as they always have when they've had to make decisions like that. But we came away from that Irish game knowing that guys were going to come through and they would be the cream of the crop in a few years time. And a lot of those guys are now.

There was never any doubt that if we were to claim a Grand Slam, the English game was going to be the big one. Ted always says, 'We've picked the best team for *this* game.' So, you were always wondering what was going to happen. You knew the England game was the massive one and you wanted to be part of that. I was fortunate enough to be in the run-on team. We played some really good footy to win 23–19. It was a funny feeling at Twickenham. They were building a new stand so the ground wasn't full. It felt weird. Tana scored the first try through DC setting him up. We led 13–10 at halftime but then Kevey scored soon after. We had a battle in the second half as England came at us. We had three guys in the sin-bin at various times — Tony Woodcock, Neemiah Tialata and Chris Masoe. So we played most of that second half with 14 guys.

At one stage we were playing with 13. Some of those refereeing decisions were just diabolical. It's always good to watch the tape afterwards and see that. But they could have ruined our Grand Slam. However, the belief in the team was outstanding. To be able to absorb all that and play with mostly 14 men was awesome. After the final whistle we definitely showed how excited we were. There were plenty of fist pumps.

We also learnt a few things from that game. We had stayed in the city and it was a long way from there out to Twickenham. We had a police escort but it was not that effective and it took us an age to get out there. Guys were starting to fall asleep in the bus. You get on the bus and you're set to go through your final preparation for the game. It's more so for the forwards, getting themselves psyched up, so it can be very frustrating when you're stuck in traffic. I think it took just over an hour to get to the game. It all meant we didn't play as well as we wanted, so we were thrilled that we'd won. Now we move hotels late in the week and we're a lot closer to Twickenham.

We now had one more game to go, against Scotland, to make the Grand Slam a reality. Despite having beaten England, I felt a bit of a let-down knowing I probably wouldn't be involved against Scotland, and I was quite keen to get home. Scotland hadn't fared too well in the Six Nations, and our side was going to be rotated again. But you always felt the guys were going to get up for that game. Yet you were still a little nervous because everyone was keen to get home and there was this last game to play. However, it was Ice's first game at fullback so I was conscious of wanting to help him out. We non-playing guys made sure that we did our bit because the players with the job to do had been helpful to us in the lead-up to the games we played. We were there to hold the shields at training and we made sure we didn't go on holiday or hit the pubs.

Those guys came out and we achieved the Grand Slam with a 29–10 victory, and it was an amazing feeling. There had been some whispers of Tana retiring, but we didn't want to believe things like that. We thought it was media speculation. He hadn't said anything about it at all. But when we were sitting in the changing rooms he announced it. He said: 'Guys, I've decided to retire from All Black rugby and I won't be playing any more internationals.' It was a sad moment. He was still in his prime, he was still playing some good footy and you knew the World Cup was only a couple of years away. And you definitely knew that T could have made it again. We said that to him but he said that his family had sacrificed too much for his rugby and now he wanted to give it back to them and to spend more time with them.

We went back to the hotel and sat in our team room a little sombre. Every person in the room said something, and there were a few tears that night. Guys were saying what they felt about his contribution to them and to the team. They thanked Tana for what he had done and how much we cared for each other and that we couldn't believe what we had done together. But the majority of it was all about T and thanking him.

It was great to be able to celebrate winning the Grand Slam and being the second New Zealand team to achieve that, especially in a centennial year. But it was also great to be able to celebrate what Tana had done for the All Blacks. In particular, from 2004 onwards when he was captain. He played a big part in shaping the way we operated as a team. He was a forceful leader, both with the coaches and the NZRU. We made some great inroads into ensuring we worked together and got on. There was a time where you didn't want to interact with the Union and officials. There was an attitude that they weren't on our side and there was some ill feeling towards them. But, as Tana pointed out, we're actually on the same team. They want to make the business side of things work for the brand and we wanted to do it all out on the field. We clashed a couple of times. There had been issues when the guys didn't really like the way things were handled. But Tana did a hell of a lot to bring us together so that we were all working on the same wavelength. For example, the players were against the haka being over-commercialised. We thought it was something really precious to All Blacks rugby and we didn't want to see it thrashed out in every bloody TV advert, just to get money. To the Union's credit, they listened.

We've also listened to where they were coming from. Because there are a lot of things they need to make the business work, and we've got to be accepting of that. As a rugby player you don't really understand how it all works unless you've been told. And I would never have dreamt of talking to chief executives before then. But Steve Tew and Jock Hobbs, the chairman, are great guys to be around. You always go and shake their hands and you want them to be part of what you've done and achieved because they are part of it. Although they're making decisions based on a business sense, they're actually part of the All Blacks. Sometimes we feel for them a bit because some of the decisions they make are not always well accepted. When they come into the team environment they could feel like they shouldn't be there, but we've accepted that they're bloody good guys and we always have a beer together.

We know full well, and respect the fact, that some of the decisions they have to make have to be made, not just for the All Blacks but for New Zealand rugby as a whole. There might be some things you don't agree with, but at the end of the day they're genuine people and they're good blokes doing what they think is best. It's a great relationship that we have now, and I think that all started with the likes of Tana and his interaction. I think both as a team, and in our relationship with the officials, we have come a long way since 2003.

Fullbacks and centres

Considering we are rivals for the fullback position **Leon MacDonald** and I get on really well. When you are an All Black you always put the team first. That's certainly been the case since Graham, Steve and Wayne have been the coaches and the rotation system has been in place. That's probably been harder for Leon to take. He's a little bit older than me and he's come through that whole environment of 'You've got to be the best in the position you play'. But no matter who you are, you can't be at your best year in, year out or even week in, week out. That was the philosophy the coaches took. But as it progressed, and the way things happened, Leon and I got on really well. We helped each other. We talked about what worked for him and what worked for me. There're areas in our games where we're probably better than each other, and where we could help each other.

I felt comfortable as the years went on that he could say that there were times in games where I should have kicked or done something differently. Initially I thought he was always hunting for my position. But when he opened up like that I trusted the fact that he really wanted to help. For a long time whenever teams were named and one or other of us was selected at fullback, we would seek each other out and shake hands. As the years went on we didn't bother because it didn't matter who was going to play. I think our relationship really grew from there.

I always looked up to Leon. When I first made the All Blacks he'd been there for a few years and I was the guy that wanted to play his position. Although he was injured I still wanted to claim that No. 15 jersey. Even now I think I am hunting him down and he probably thinks the same way. But it's good competition; it's not a backstabbing rivalry. It's not something where people say one thing to you and then something to someone else. It's never been like that with Leon. I think he's contributed to getting the best out of me by both helping and then providing healthy competition. We don't keep things from each other. If we can help each other then the team's going to succeed. And if the team's going to succeed then we all succeed.

Our coaches have really driven the idea that no one is ever going to be better than the team. And you always hear those clichés in team environments that 'There's no "I" in team', or 'Team before self', and so on. But they really hit home, especially when we went through the rotation stage. No one was ever better than the team. It didn't matter who you were, how high up you were or how experienced you were. You'd always put the team before yourself. And that probably helped our relationship as fullbacks.

We still have a healthy rivalry in the Super 14 where you keep an eye on what your opponent is doing during the competition. I have watched Leon play throughout the Super 14 and because his Crusaders team has traditionally played well that provided me with more incentive to keep on my toes. Whenever the Chiefs play the Crusaders it creates an extra challenge. You want to go out and give it your best. But we always have a decent laugh after the games, whoever's won. There is that wee bit of an edge to it, because you're playing against him. But you don't go out and trash talk your way through. Fullbacks don't do things like that anyway, we don't go out there and purposely want to trash each other or injure each other. But you do have to bring your A-game, and hopefully play better. I probably put more emphasis on that when we play the Crusaders. I've got to be better than Leon. No doubt he is doing the same. He's probably got it over me, the last five or six years, so that doesn't help at all.

There is sledging out on the field but I don't indulge in it myself. When I first started with Auckland and we played Canterbury that was the only time I've heard heavy sledging going on between Carlos Spencer, Justin Marshall and Andrew Mehrtens. I couldn't get over it. I was only 21, and when I heard these guys going at it I was shocked — and amused. It involved a mixture of humour and insult. I didn't understand the relationship those guys had. I think it was more insults between Los and Marshie, whereas Mehrts and Los were probably joking around a lot.

I'm not a big fan of sledging. You hear it now and then. But I don't hear it as much as the front row does. There's always one guy that's going to be an idiot and go at it. I think South Africans are really fond of that when it comes to scrum time. I just can't believe they've got time to sledge. Some South African boys line up and say, 'We're going to scrum you into the ground.' I'd laugh my head off if someone said stuff like that.

There was one incident in 2008 that sticks in my mind. It proved a big motivation in our success. Of course, it involved an Australian. They can't help themselves. We shared the incident as a team going into the

Brisbane game when it was 1–1 with two to play. But a win would mean we would keep the Bledisloe Cup. There will be no surprises that it was Matt Dunning who was involved. After we lost the first game in Sydney he walked past some of the boys and said, 'We are going to beat you 3–0.' And Lote Tuqiri also commented, 'We're going to take the Bledisloe Cup off you.' Then, after we beat the Springboks in Cape Town, we were out that night and the Australians had just arrived for their game the following week, and while we were having a few beers at a club they carried on about how they were going to take the Cup off us. That just lit a big fire under us.

What really got to us was Dunning's comment. He hadn't even started, he'd come off the bench and he was Matt Dunning. He didn't even contribute that much in the game. I'm not saying all the Aussies are like that. But that one comment really pissed a lot of guys off, and it didn't help that he had said it to Ali Williams. Ali doesn't hold back. He told the boys, and we knew that in Brisbane there would be no way they were going take the Cup off us. It was also the fact that they were making statements like that so early in the competition. They'd beaten us in one game and were already contemplating taking the silverware off us, and beating us three-nil. Not 2–1 but 3–0. Matt's an interesting character and the fact that he's not a world-class prop, who managed to hang around for so long because there was no one else coming through for the Aussies, made his comment all the more unacceptable. I see they're starting to bring some guys through now so he might not be there for much longer.

It is harder to mix with opposing sides nowadays. I know they used to do it a lot back in the earlier years but there's now so much focus on recovery and getting back to the hotel and eating and going to bed. On the occasions when we do go out and there's a designated club that we go to, we do mix. We have a laugh together and we talk. We don't talk rugby, we just go there and have some laughs really. I think every rugby player understands you've got to let your hair down a little here and there. If you don't, it makes you look like an arrogant type, I believe. It's always good to say, 'Gidday guys.'

You know there's always going to be that battle on the field, but there's no use playing the game on Thursday when you're going out for dinner. When the game comes around that's when you go hard. But when you're off the field and you're having a good time you always catch up and have a decent drink together. I think that's probably where it differs a lot from the corporate world, where you probably wouldn't mix much with your competition, unless you really knew them. So, it's great to be able to meet opposing teams socially, and you do make a lot of mates that way. You're not really close mates but you do catch up with them a lot. I think the South Africans are really good like that too.

In terms of fullback opponents other than Leon, one I really rate is **Isaia Toeava**. I took Ice under my wing somewhat when he first came along. He was 19 years old but I knew then he had the goods to be a superstar of the game. He could easily pick one of second-five, centre or fullback one day and say, 'Right, I'm going to be the man in that position.' Now he's starting to realise that fullback might be that choice. I think ultimately it will be either fullback or centre. I know he's only 22 but one day he's going to explode. He's got the nous, he's strong for his age, he's fast and he's good on his feet. He's one of those kids you see when you're watching an Under-9s game — the one who's always beating players. He's the one kid who stands out. He's so talented that he doesn't even know it himself.

He's faced a lot of criticism because he didn't blossom straight away. Whether that was a maturity thing or he didn't have any confidence in himself I don't know. At 19 I wonder whether you'd ever have enough confidence in yourself, especially a shy Samoan boy. I've seen the way he trains and the way his body is, and the things he can do, and I believe he's got the goods to be a world-class player. The only thing he has to work on is his mental side. One dropped ball to him is a bloody disaster. The game's over, and he's had a terrible game. But that's the way the game pans out. It's inevitable you're going to make more than one mistake. However, he struggles to let that go, and keeps thinking about it. He is able to come off the field and tell me how many balls he dropped, then how he dropped it. That was the only thing he'd focused on. To some extent I'd probably play with his head a little in a humorous way because he's still vying for my position. But I'm always trying to give him advice and getting him to concentrate on the simple things. When he played in the Bledisloe Cup game in Hong Kong, I rang and texted him and said, 'Don't worry about anything else, just concentrate on the basic things. Start there and build your way through.' And he was really stoked, I think it lifted him. After I took Ice under my wing they started calling him my son and he became known as Junior.

Cory Jane is another who is coming through now. In the past I regarded him as a developing fullback. But he has advanced from that and he is one of those players who really expresses himself. He's probably the opposite of Ice in that it doesn't matter how many mistakes he makes, he'll still keep having a crack. He reminds me a lot of how Christian Cullen used to play, especially in the way he runs. He's not a big boy but he's deceptive. He's another one who has made the All Blacks now and I think the hardest thing for new players is to go back and really try to light that flame again with their sides in order to make the All Blacks every year. Cory's certainly got the goods to do that. He didn't get much time overseas in 2008, but certainly for the Hurricanes he's a guy you definitely have to look out for. And he's got a big future. He's a little bit older than Ice but he's definitely a tidy player.

Zac Guildford and **Israel Dagg** are others to watch. I looked at Israel Dagg two or three years ago and thought, 'Far out, this kid's going to be good. I've got to watch him.' And I thought he might have progressed a lot faster than Zac did. Zac was in the Hurricanes a lot earlier but Israel's move to the Highlanders will be his chance. It will not surprise me if he is knocking on the door soon.

So there's a lot of talent coming through. That's the beauty about New Zealand. They talk about the player drain and everyone leaving, but that's always going to happen. Our age group level is phenomenal in the way it brings players through, at Under-19s, or at New Zealand Secondary Schools. It is amazing how dominant we are in those grades on the world stage. As time goes on, guys are always going to leave, but there will always be that real talent coming through. It's going to keep New Zealand healthy so long as they can keep age grade rugby really competitive.

A scary thing for players heading overseas is that a year down the track people can forget who you are. Take Chris Jack for example. He was *the* lock, but no sooner was he gone than all of a sudden they're talking Brad Thorn and they've almost forgotten who Chris Jack is. You still want to be an All Black until that one day when you get told that you're not going to be it again. I cringe when I think that day might come soon and I will have to give it all up. But I've always believed I'd always want the All Black jersey to be the be-all and end-all of everything in rugby. I've perhaps lessened my thoughts on that, with maturity and a family now. There are other things in life, but that pull of the jersey is definitely still there.

And then there was Cully, **Christian Cullen**. I think everything he touched turned to gold. The way he ran, and defended, was sensational. There's no doubt his time in the All Blacks jersey was cut short. And there is equally no doubt that his misfortune was my gain. But Christian Cullen was probably the best fullback in the world of all time. The way he played the game, his attacking ability and the way he ran, coupled with his great strength, made him outstanding. He wasn't very big but he broke tackles with sheer explosive speed. Guys fell off him and he ran great angles. He'd never think twice about running certain angles, and I'd never see myself running angles like that. He ran a short line that came off the player with the ball. He would come off a centre, and hit it at such pace. Whether he was going to get wasted or not he would hit that line at 100 miles an hour.

Because I played centre, it was my natural inclination to wait and try to create something for someone other than myself. That was one aspect of my game that I really struggled to try and get to: running a short line, running an out line or running a squarer line. It took me ages to do that. When I came on against Munster in 2008 and passed to Joe Rokocoko, who scored the match-winning try, that was an example of being able to do it at just the right time.

Earlier in my career I would never have done something like that. It's probably one of the downfalls of shifting between centre and fullback. At centre you're trying to create gaps for your wings, while at fullback you are looking to run into gaps at speed by hitting off the centres, just like the wings do. I was aware that I needed to be able to do that at fullback and spoke to Wayne Smith a lot about it, but he always reassured me that I didn't need to do that. Smithy always said Cully was a different player who wanted to score tries. It was my goal to be giving the last pass to Joe or Dougie to score. But a part of me felt like I still failed to do it the way Cully had. Playing fullback more regularly did help to be able to work on those little things. Even when playing centre I was trying to be like Tana Umaga and hit off the second five-eighths and then be able to come back out and fend off a hooker like Tana did for the Hurricanes against the Crusaders one year when Mark Hammett was given the old 'don't argue' from Tana as he raced through. I also found it hard to one week be trying to work on perfecting my game at centre and then the next having to work on my fullback's game. And as the game kept changing I found I had to be able to kick better because I needed to be able to kick back over the opposition winger's head when they had kicked to us. It was a constantly changing set of circumstances, but hopefully I adapted well.

Among the fullbacks I have played against, **Chris Latham** has been a good rival and I always enjoyed the contest. I never got the chance to speak to him that much. I was always hesitant to swap jerseys and never did that with him. I always knew how good I would have to be to outplay him. While he's overseas now, he was always one who had me on my game. What makes Latham different is his kicking ability: he can kick long, decent punts and he is an unorthodox player. You think he is going to kick and then he runs. Before you know it he is breaking through the whole team. He had an ability to create something when you didn't think it was going to happen.

Mat Rogers was awesome when he first came on the scene. He probably got dragged into that centre-second five-fullback sort of scenario and before you knew it he was on the bench and wasn't even getting game time. He was another who I had grown up watching play league, so for that reason it was great to play against him. Rogers always had intelligence and attacking flair, although I think he probably struggled a little with union. In spite of that I always believed he was the goods. The way he ran the ball back and beat players was awesome to watch.

Another player I admired was **Matthew Burke**. He was also someone I'd watched while growing up. Then all of a sudden I was playing against him. He was a very good goal kicker and he was fast. He was big, and rarely made mistakes. He and **Joe Roff** — Joe obviously played wing a lot more — were excellent players. Matthew was always there at the right time, and made really good decisions, and when that was to have a go, nine times out of 10 he would make the break. If he or Joe didn't break, they would take the more conservative, but often correct, choice of 'Let's not do something too stupid to turn the ball over'. They were awesome at that, and to a certain extent I wanted to be that sort of player: I didn't really want to make too many mistakes or chance my arm as often as perhaps I should. I just wanted to play safe.

South Africa's **Percy Montgomery** was another I looked up to as a young player and I was honoured to play against him. That was especially the case when he played his 100th game, in the 2008 Tri Nations. He was a decent guy, not the biggest bloke in the world, but he had a big heart and loved the game and he always wanted to swap jerseys and shorts and I couldn't get over that. I thought the first time was amazing. He came up to me in the dressing room and said, 'Hey, Mils, do you want to swap?' I was humbled. To have played against him I would have given my jersey to him without exchanging. But we swapped. And then we played again and he wanted to swap again. Now I've got a whole heap of Springbok No. 15 jerseys with Percy Montgomery's name on them.

But I refused to swap his 100th jersey. I gave him my strip that day. I went and saw him after the game and caught him in the hallway and I said, 'Thanks, Percy, it's been a pleasure playing your 100th game and well done, it's been awesome.' And he said, 'No, no, no, I'll have to swap with you, I'll give you my other one.' And I said, 'No, it's yours mate, you've achieved that, it's a massive milestone and it's all yours.' He was taken aback by it. I was glad I did that and to see his reaction. I've got a lot of respect for Percy and the things that he's achieved with two World Cup wins. It was great watching him as an aspiring rugby player and then to be able to play against him. Sometimes you have got to pinch yourself because you can't believe you're playing these guys.

I don't swap jerseys very often. I'm pretty hesitant about going into the opposition dressing rooms. I always wanted to swap with Chris Latham but I was reluctant to go in and swap with him. I hoped that he would come and ask me. But there was the time in 2006 in Brisbane when I played centre and Stirling Mortlock asked me if I wanted to swap and I jumped at that. That's the only Aussie jersey I have swapped. He came into the changing rooms after the game and we had a beer together and swapped jerseys. Early on in my career I didn't swap a lot because you always treasure those jerseys. When you've got your first one, you never give that away. Then as your appearances mount you've still got people you want to give jerseys to. Family members and the church and others. Some would ask to swap but I would have to say I couldn't because I had promised it to someone else. But now that I have played a fair number of games I am at the stage where I'm starting to want the other jerseys now.

But there are things you have to watch out for. The likes of the English, they get two jerseys and one of them is not embroidered. I got caught out with that in the English game where Ben Cohen wanted to swap with me in Auckland. I gladly did so but then found out later it was his other jersey and I was gutted. So, ever since then, when someone's offered to exchange I've always asked if that's the jersey with their name embroidered on it. That way when I take it home it doesn't look like I've gone out and bought it. If they've got their name and the date on it, it makes them a bit special.

Among the centres I've played against **Stirling Mortlock** was up there. He's the guy who all the Australians turn to. When they're down, all of a sudden he stands up and the whole team rallies around him and lifts. He's the one guy who can do that for the Brumbies, or for the Aussies. If you know Stirlo's on his game and he lifts, he can change the game. He did that in Melbourne in 2007. A couple of cracking runs and before you knew it there were 14 other players around him. He hits a hole, or he makes a big tackle. He's the guy that you want to shut down and not let do too much. And you can't just shut him down for the first five or 10 minutes, you've got to make it last. Because if you don't he'll stand up. He's a leader. He leads by example. He's a really good guy off the field as well.

Of course, **Tana Umaga** was another one. He's one of the great All Black centres. I learnt a lot from him both on and off the field, and I always looked up to him because of who he was. He was an All Black captain but he also had a Samoan background and you could relate to some of the things he was saying. We said when he left that we were really humbled to serve under him. And that's the way we felt: we were serving him. If he asked us to do something it was never something he couldn't do himself. And that's what I admired about T. He also stood up for his players. There were times when he stuck his neck out for the guys with coaches and officialdom. When guys weren't happy about certain things he would voice that frustration. It's hard in any situation to be able to voice your opinions and concerns about what's wrong. But he was really strong with that and if someone wasn't pulling his weight or if there was something about the management that the boys weren't happy with he would voice his opinion strongly. Sometimes he might come back after being told 'No, you can't have that'. But at least he did it. You knew you had a captain who generally cared for your feedback and your opinion and how a team was going to be run.

Gareth Thomas was a pretty good opponent. He was something of a go-to player for Wales. He was similar in style to Mortlock, but Stirlo probably had more impact in a game. Thomas played fullback as well. I always enjoyed playing the northern hemisphere guys. He was another one that you knew you had to watch out for.

I always rated **Jamie Noon**. I think he's really solid, very stable. He's probably got a little caught in that trap where they're rotating a bit more and has been caught out coming back from injury. But I've always thought he was a decent centre, and very strong. The game over there is a lot different to how we play. They are more concerned about physicality, whereas here in New Zealand, and the southern hemisphere generally, our centres have more flair and we mix it up more. I think their mentality is just crash-bash. They don't seem to be as preoccupied as we are with using the ball.

Northern hemisphere teams, especially the English, have the thought that they've got to win the physical contest above everything else and that will be enough to win the game. But there's a lot more than that to winning. Of course you want to win the physical dominance and the physical battle, that's the way the All Blacks have always been. But there are times when you have to realise you can't go to only one place to beat them, and when that's not working you have to change to something else. You have to be able to exploit different skills of the game. It's not a case of 'I'm going to run it straight at you and recycle the ball as fast as I can, and then another guy's going to run straight at you'. There are other skills required. Some say that the northern hemisphere game is just a 10-man game where they just bash and kick, bash and kick, whereas New Zealand teams look for other options. The Super 14 has a reputation as a flashy sort of tournament where you run everything. But that is simplifying it too much. You don't run everything, but when you compare the Super 14 and Heineken Cup tournaments I definitely know which one I'd prefer to watch. I have heard Byron Kelleher say that the two tournaments are equal. I suppose that is a marketing ploy. And he is playing at the top end of the Heineken Cup where the expectations are greater.

I think the criticism that northern hemisphere sides don't know how to pass the ball is right. They've gone away and just worked on gym, gym, gym, and I don't know whether that's because of the weather or that they just want to crash and bash. We found that when Warren Gatland came back to Waikato he wanted to play that way. He wanted us to be really physical. I don't know what it is. They've got a lot of talent out wide but they just seem to want to win the physicality battle at the cost of being able to move the ball as fluently as they used to. The South Africans used to be like that but they are changing. They've come on in leaps and bounds in the way they play their game now with the expansiveness of it all. They let the ball go a little, which is a response, I suppose, to the way the laws have panned out and the game has changed.

Collision in Cardiff

When the pre-World Cup conditioning programme was first mentioned to us there were a lot of guys who didn't agree with it, but again we committed to it. We knew that we had to. It was thought to be best for the team and all the studies seemed to say that you needed to keep guys training and then build them up so they were peaking at the right time. It was hard because we had never done it before, and we were heading into unknown territory. We didn't know how we were going to come out the other end and whether it would work or not. We were putting our faith in sports science.

We sat down and worked out our goals, what we wanted to sacrifice through the year and how we were going to go about doing that. The programme devised was probably the hardest training I had ever done bar the New Zealand Sevens. People didn't really see how hard you were working but it was twice a day and just as hard, if not harder, than the guys in the Super 14 did. However, you were not getting the reward of being able to play in the weekends, and I think that was probably the hardest thing to take. It felt great to be getting rested and stronger. I knew I was feeling faster and fitter, but the satisfaction of being able to get out there and play the games was missing.

We were not going to be involved again until rounds six or seven of the Super 14, but by then I had my own issues with a hamstring injury. Then the week before I was due back I played in a warm-up game and broke my foot, which set me back again. It was a frustrating time. I was that close to being able to get out there and get some value for all the training that I had been doing for the last three or so months. It was all pretty disappointing and in the end it felt like a really long holiday. In the last phase of it I couldn't even run. But I was fortunate enough to get back out there to play the Chiefs' last two games of the season and we had a shot at making the semi-finals. But in the end we were dependent on other results which didn't go our way and that was disappointing. On reflection, though, it is my belief that we were probably a year too late with the reconditioning. We probably should have done it the year before.

Hindsight is a pretty good thing and a lot of guys reaped the rewards of the reconditioning the year after the World Cup in 2008. I think the reconditioning was probably a little bit long, but who was to know that? It would have been great to be sitting here and saying that a reconditioning window was the perfect thing and that's what won us the World Cup, but unfortunately that was a hard lesson to have to take. All the effort and sacrifices we put in place were not enough on the day that we lost to the French. I thought the reconditioning itself was a good concept. We did need more than a month's rest. The constant diet of starting in January and not finishing until the end of November had taken its toll over the years. It gets quite gruelling on your body and if you want to get the best out of yourself I think you definitely need more than the month's rest or time off that we were getting.

We didn't lack any motivation during that period because we knew it was the World Cup year. So you are more inclined to go back to starting your training a lot earlier than you would have in the past. Everyone's training programme was different. My focus was to get fitter and bigger in order to cope with playing two or three kilos heavier with muscle rather than fat. My memory is of having to get up every day for two trainings a day whether it was out on the field or in the gym. They were hard sessions and we only had a month off after that massive tour of the UK.

What people don't realise is that although you have been given a month off, it's not a full month of doing absolutely nothing. It might be a week off from all activity but then you've almost got to start again and start training and getting that base fitness back before you present yourself as ready to start the real hard stuff. You have three weeks building up and two weeks of that solid training before you start back in the team training programmes. That's where your body still takes a lot of hammering. You obviously have an impact with your running or your gym work but by doing that you are probably not getting over some of the injuries you may have lingering from the year before. What you really want is to get away from it and have some time off to be able to nurse those injuries and get physio on them. That's where I believe you need a whole month off before you start the two weeks of training by yourself to get that base fitness and then go into fitness testing. That's what we are missing at the moment. Guys' careers are not going to be as long because they are picking up more soft tissue injuries than perhaps they did in the past.

But the build-up to the World Cup itself was fantastic. France didn't do us any favours by sending out a third-string team. However, we still had to do the job against them, and we managed that 42–11 in Auckland and 61–10 in Wellington. But I didn't play in those two games as I was still getting over my injury. I came back to play 60-odd minutes in the 64–13 win over Canada. I felt fine and was able to play at fullback again in the 26–21 win over South Africa in Durban. The 15–20 loss we suffered in Melbourne to Australia felt like a hiccup. It was one of those games where no one talked. We got to the hard stages, a place we hadn't been in for a long time, with situations where we were down and things weren't working for us, the game plan wasn't working, we weren't getting feedback and guys weren't talking. Someone needed to be saying, 'We've got to try something different.' We hadn't been put under that pressure over the previous three or so years. Everything had gone smoothly bar that game in Wales. We hadn't had to think about being put under that pressure of needing to appreciate we had to try to change tack. It was also my 50th test, so it was a game I definitely remember, but we still had the belief that we were a lot better than them. I don't know what it was.

Stirling Mortlock made a couple of great breaks, one of them leading to a try that really put the nail in the coffin for us, and we were gutted. But even after the second try we had the feeling that we could still come back and beat them. There was a thought in the back of your mind that there were better things to come with the World Cup and we just wanted to get the Tri Nations out of the way. Because that was all everyone was talking about. We had a slip-up in Melbourne. There was a thought about whether something like that might happen at the World Cup but we just wanted to get past that loss, win the Tri Nations, and the Bledisloe Cup, and then get onto the really good stuff. The loss meant we had plenty of motivation to win the Tri Nations and we did by beating South Africa

33–6 in Christchurch and then Australia 26–12 in Auckland.

The Auckland game was our last hit out before the World Cup team was to be named the next day. Despite the win there were no guarantees of selection and everyone was waiting to see if they were going to be named. When we went back to the hotel we found out a few guys had already been given their talking to and told they were not going. I was shocked when I heard about Piri Weepu and then Troy Flavell missing out. You always feel for guys like that, you get so close to them and when they get told they are not going to make the team it is tough, but more so when it is a World Cup.

But I think Piri learnt from that. If he was to look back now and say what he had done wrong, he would have definitely changed a lot of things. It was a lesson to all of us because you know that could be you at any given stage. During the conditioning window in our last camp we were given awards and Piri won an award for losing the most weight. He had worked really hard but then went back into Super 14 and back to himself. I am sure he learnt from that because he played some really good footy in 2008. I actually picked up the award for the guy who put on the most muscle in the team. That was pleasing. I felt like I had done something right in my training.

When the World Cup team was named we went to Eden Park in our number ones. I had a sense of 2003 being not that long ago. But, in reverse, back in 2004, it seemed a long, long time until 2007 and the chance that would provide for winning the Cup. The excitement about the task ahead was certainly there and we knew we really had to get things right. We were in such a good space that we'd done everything right and all was in place. We had won everything for the last three or so years and we were the favourites.

Our pool wasn't as hard as it might have been. In some respects we weren't put under the pressure that perhaps we wanted, and needed, to be under. You can't train in that sort of pressure. Anything that you do on the training paddock is not the same as some of the pressure that you are put under when you are, say, three points down and you've got to come back and you've got to score. Five metres out from the line with 15 minutes to go and you need to win the game — that's the sort of pressure you want to work in. But when you are winning by 50 or 40-odd points, I mean even the Scotland game we won by 40 points, it is hard to get the sorts of scenarios you need.

In our first game, against Italy, we put ourselves under more pressure than the Italians could. We spoke about that and how we had to get even the smallest things right. We were prepared to experiment a little in hitting different channels and what outcomes were going to come from those phases. We started the tournament with a hiss and a roar. Being the first game we just wanted to explode and we did that. There was a period, very early in the game, where we knew we were going to win and win convincingly. We had to try and I suppose simulate some way of putting pressure on ourselves; whether it was the way we cleaned out or got faster to a breakdown or being more efficient at a breakdown or in defence.

We set those as goals for the game because we had to try to be able to match the pressure stronger teams would put us under. When you are playing a team like Australia and you are in a ruck you expect to get hit harder and there are going to be guys going in lower and in better body positions. You know if you are playing the Portuguese, they are going to have all the best intentions but they are going to be a lot higher and they are going to try to wrestle you to the ground. But you are going to have better body position and tactically they are not going to be as good as the likes of an Australian or English team where they can manipulate you and put you under pressure when you are on defence. The Portuguese didn't offer anything on attack. But that isn't an excuse because we knew that was going to happen and we were not alone in having to cope with those differences in playing standards. All the top teams faced the same problems. Except perhaps Ireland, France and Argentina who were drawn in the same pool.

Our base in Marseille was great. We knew we were at the World Cup. There was a lot better feeling and more hype about the World Cup than there was when we were in Melbourne in 2003. We were welcomed, we had a reception there with the mayor and they embraced us Kiwis, and All Blacks, especially. It was a great spot to be in. Everything was laid on for us and we really appreciated their hospitality. A couple of years before we wanted to get onside with the French people so that if they weren't cheering for the French then we wanted them to be cheering for the All Blacks. We did things like going to the soccer and wearing the French shirts. We really went out there to try to promote that All Black brand. We did things like going to Stade Français and training while wearing their pink outfits. There was a limited edition sale of those pink polos and they were gone within half an hour. I think it just got the French thinking about the All Blacks more and we did have a big support base in France. They actually loved the All Blacks. There were reports that the highest selling replica jerseys were All Blacks jerseys.

We wanted to be able to have that crowd behind us if we weren't playing the French. Looking at the draw, we hoped we wouldn't meet them until much later than we did and unfortunately we know that day we met them at the wrong time. But our approach to those early games worked. For instance, against Portugal in Lyon, it was outstanding. What happened was that those teams were taken aback about us not being precious with them. We adopted our 'yes attitude' and got into it. After games we would go into their changing rooms and have a beer with them and ask them how they were going and they were surprised by that too. They said to us that we had to win the tournament because of the way we spoke with them. For them it had been an experience on its own to play the All Blacks but to be able to have a beer and a chat afterwards made their day. I think if you have a team like Portugal playing one of the big guns of world rugby it's going to be special for them and you have to remember that it is a World Cup where there are teams taking part who are on the fringe of the game. When they got that drop kick over and the stadium erupted, you know they felt like they had won the game and it felt good for us too. That's what rugby is all about.

When a small rugby nation like Portugal can come out and be so passionate about scoring, it is terrific and great to see rugby making its mark in those parts of the world. Although we gave them a decent hiding their supporters were fantastic and I think ours learnt something from them as well. It was a great, great afternoon. It's not often you experience a standing ovation when you've given the other team a hiding. But to use a cliché, rugby was the winner at the end of the day, it definitely was.

Moving to Scotland exposed us to different weather, certainly a lot different to the south of France. It was a difficult few days there for me because I had been injured in the first couple of minutes of the Portugal game and I was more looking ahead to the last pool game against Romania in Toulouse. We did have an issue with the jerseys looking the same, but overall it was a good week and the 40–0 win was another step on the way. I think once you get to that stage, it was the third game of the tour, and in any tour the third and fourth weeks can be the hardest unless you've got some sort of motivation to kick on. There was a feeling that we were just waiting around for the next game before getting into the real work.

We went back to Aix-en-Provence after the Scotland game and were given a couple of days off. That's probably the first trip I ever really enjoyed being on. I mean it helped that Hayley was there and we got out and spent time looking around different buildings and vineyards and experienced some of the food, which I had never done before. I thoroughly enjoyed being away from rugby for a few days. It was really exciting to get time away and take in some of the world. On other tours I'd always be stuck in my room thinking about rugby and nothing else. A few guys went to Monaco and other places but we decided to stay in Aix. It was very pleasant, a student town, but with lots of history, and little streets that you wander around, which was all very relaxing. We had great weather and biked everywhere. We went into Marseille and really enjoyed the break.

The coaches' mentality was that after three or four weeks on tour we needed some motivation. There was criticism about that but we definitely appreciated it in the end because it was starting to be a little bit draining. I know it didn't sound like much, three or so weeks compared to what they used to do back in the old days, but everything is just full on the whole week and then you've got one day to recover and then it's full on again. That's what you want to try to get away from, so we did appreciate getting a couple of days off.

It was decided I wouldn't risk myself in the Romanian game in Toulouse. But I gave my hammy a decent work out after the Romanian game and then we were off to Cardiff. Being a quarter-final we knew the build-up was going to be awesome. This was what we really wanted, this was what those four preliminary games had been all about, getting to this game. And the next three games we hoped to play were the big ones. Each was a little bit closer to being in the World Cup final.

We got to Cardiff the next day, and while wandering round there was that sense again of 'Am I going to be picked, or am I not?' I felt it was going to be 50/50 given the fact that Leon was playing so well, I had been injured and I had only played one game at centre and then about two minutes at fullback. I was thinking along the lines of fullback and that it would be touch and go whether I would make the team or be on the bench that weekend. So again it was a case of trying to avoid the coach as best I could. But at training, Ted must have cottoned on to that and I saw him walking over to me. My heart was in my mouth. I was thinking I was going to be given the word that I wouldn't be starting. He came up and said, 'Thirteen.' I had only been thinking about fullback. I never thought I would be playing centre. After telling me that he smiled and asked: 'Is that all right?' and I said, 'That's fine.' I was stoked; I was actually going to be in the starting 15, so I sort of jogged away.

I think Leon must have seen him talk to me and he asked me what had happened and I said I was playing centre. It was a bit of a shock, but I was determined. I was ready to put my hand up and that whole week was awesome. I wouldn't change anything about our preparation. I felt we had a really good week and the intensity we had at training and the things we did at training were great.

We were out of Cardiff at the Welsh training centre at the Vale, a golf resort. We had lost the toss at the manager's meeting for the choice of hotels so we were not going to get the hotel we preferred, which was the Hilton in the middle of Cardiff. If I could change one thing it would probably be that. It had shades of the game that we played against the

English where we were staying a long way away from Twickenham and guys had started to fall asleep on the way to the ground. But everything else, the whole preparation, the whole week, was just great.

I wouldn't change anything in terms of what we did on the training pitch and how we trained. During our training for the World Cup pool games we were also learning the new game plan as well. This quarter-final was going to be the start of the game plan that we'd wanted to learn. Everything else that we had done in the pool games was our old game plan. But at training that week we were learning a different plan. This was going to be our first game against some really good opposition. You looked at the French and the way they were going in the tournament but you knew they were really unpredictable. You were aware they could go through a tournament as they had done, losing the opening game to Argentina, yet all of a sudden they could come out with all guns blazing. And as we now know we played probably the poorest rugby we had ever played.

With time, and reflection, I think the fact we were trying a new game plan at that stage was a factor. We probably concentrated too much on 'It's going to come, it's going to come.' We felt it would eventually work but that places where we were trying to attack would not open up. We started going into one-off runners and keeping it really tight. It was a case of let's keep it, one-off, one-off, one-off and eventually we'll break them. But that didn't happen. Although I haven't ever watched the game, I can recall there were spaces down the blindside that we didn't exploit because we were so fixed on the game plan. We probably lost a little bit of our attacking nous that day. We didn't have our attacking flair and were unable to chance our arm and explore different things. We were so set on bashing out this game plan which we always believed was going to work.

Clearly it didn't. And no one stood up and said, 'This isn't working, let's go back to something different.' That was probably our downfall in the end because we had always believed it was good for us and we believed in what we were doing. That probably hardened us in the view that it was the way to go. But no one thought, 'No, this isn't working, we've got to change.' And I suppose that was the lesson we hadn't absorbed from the game we lost to Australia in Melbourne.

When you look at some of the statistical analysis that was done on our game, it is revealing. When our quarter-final loss to France was compared with our 47–3 win over them nearly a year earlier, it showed how much more definitive we had been in our execution in the 2006 game. We scored seven tries and had only 43 rucks while kicking the ball 29 times. We made only 91 passes in the game. But in the quarter-final, we had 165 rucks! It was believed to be the highest number of rucks in any test match in rugby history. But knockout rugby can cause these things to happen. The same statistical study showed that France, which had beaten England in a pre-World Cup 'friendly', had kicked the ball only 19 times. Yet in its semi-final against England a week after beating us, it kicked the ball 46 times and lost. The statistics showed there was an average of 55 kicks in test matches, but the semi-finals had 86 and 85 kicks respectively, while the final had 91.

In the midst of our inability to seal the quarter-final we didn't say, 'Hey, let's try something different', whether it was a downfield kick to put some pressure on and sit in the 22 for a while and pick up the points. We thought that if we just kept going down that same channel eventually things would open up. But, as the game went on and it wasn't working, the more we went into our shells. Then it only took one mistake from us for them to be able to go down there, and then one mistake from the bloody ref not to pick up the forward pass and the swing of the game had gone their way, and all they were really doing was hanging on.

What we were trying to do was win the bloody thing, but the chances of trying to hang on are a lot higher when you are up against a really decent team, and you could see the French lift. At one stage we were five metres out and we tried to keep picking and going and we ended up losing the ball. The French got it, kicked it out and then they lifted again.

We made breaks a couple of times. Nick Evans broke and I went through in support. He passed it low and I tried to pick it up instead of kicking it. I would have scored. It's weird. You think about those sorts of moments afterwards and you know its moments like those that win you the game. And then, all of a sudden, it doesn't. Everything starts deteriorating. I went away from that game thinking, 'What the hell, why didn't I just kick it, why didn't I just kick it, why didn't I just kick it?' You would give anything to go back to that moment. That will probably be the only thing I will remember from that game: that we could have won if we'd just done that or whatever. I always believed that we could go on and win that World Cup and when it got down to that final minute or so, I still sort of believed that.

Back at the hotel no one talked, no one said anything. All the partners came round, but it was like a funeral. Everyone was down and we just couldn't believe it. I remember going into dinner and sitting down and trying to make conversation. I said to Keith Robertson, 'Have you heard from your kids?' because all the fathers had missed their kids and Keith said, 'Yeah, I spoke to them.' And I said he would be getting to see them this weekend. He just about broke down. He was hurting. Everyone was.

We just went and had a few beers and tried to drown our sorrows. We perhaps had more beers than we needed to. That helped for a little while

I suppose but we always knew the next day was going to come and that it was time to get home. Darren Shand was busting his arse off to try to find flights home for everyone because we didn't have any arranged. Not that we all wanted to jump on a flight to go home. It wasn't as if everyone was putting up their hands to be on that first flight out.

We had a meeting the next day about how things were at home. We needed to front the media and that was going to be tough to take. We went and did the job and that was probably when I broke down. I just couldn't believe that we had lost. It was like reality finally starting to sink in. I remember hiding underneath a table with Neemiah Tialata and Ice just so I wouldn't get noticed. It was hard to revisit it again and the disbelief was constant. I was a wreck. It was the culmination of so much. I thought I had done everything right, and I'd sacrificed a lot to get to there.

When we arrived home our reception showed me that New Zealand as a whole had really matured. People came and said, 'Never mind.' We couldn't believe it. The guys who came back early had 2000 people meet them. Those of us who had stayed behind because we couldn't make that flight were amazed too. When we said goodbye to those guys, it was like 'Good luck, you guys are going to cop it'. But when we read about it on the Internet and saw the reaction we were overwhelmed. New Zealanders had grown up and there was only a minority who were not happy. It was fantastic to have New Zealanders come up to you and say, 'Oh, don't worry about what happened.' But that didn't make the defeat any easier to take.

It took me ages to get over it. I had to get back in the bloody saddle eventually. Hayley did a really good job of that in what was a difficult time. We did try to talk about it later as a group but it was a tough time for everyone and it was a case of just trying to forget it as best we could and moving on. There was a debrief of all the senior guys when we got home about what had actually occurred, or trying to understand what had happened. I think the NZRU were trying to make a decision as to whether or not they were going to sack the coach. There were phone calls and email exchanges. There was an option to put your name on the email form and I put my name on it. It didn't bother me at all what I had said and I firmly believed that I had been coached by the best coaching staff and it wasn't their fault we had lost. I couldn't pick anything that had been wrong.

I came home and went through a tough month. Hayley had got me on a plane to get me out of Hamilton, out of the garage where I was drowning my sorrows just about every second day. She knew I had to get out of there so she flew us down to Invercargill to spend some time with my family, which was probably the best thing that she'd ever done. I think she rang Gilbert to ask what she could do because I was just so despondent. I didn't want to be around anyone. But then when we were down south Steve Cottrell rang me about it which reminded me of it again. By then I'd started to heal a little and I gave him feedback on what I thought had happened and how things were. There wasn't one thing we lacked. The travelling was all fine, the timing of events was fine. You couldn't fault any of the preparation. There was nothing you could put your finger on and say, 'This was why we lost.' It just came down to us not performing on the day. It's hard to say that you didn't perform. As All Blacks we always said we were not just there to play and perform, we always wanted to beat teams by 20 points.

We knew that there would always be a sack-the-coach response. I felt for Ted. It's harder for coaches when teams aren't going that well. I suppose it would have been all right if he was a prick, or he wasn't a decent coach. But given what happened in the last two World Cups you always knew the writing was on the wall and there would be a public reaction with the knives out and giving it to them.

As a player you started to weigh up your options about who was going to be the coach, whether it was Ted or Robbie Deans. Robbie was so loved by his Canterbury and Crusaders supporters, who obviously wanted to get rid of Ted. I remember thinking Ted needed another year. Despite the World Cup disappointment I knew we were still going to be successful. I had the belief that time would heal and as it's turned out now that's exactly how it stands. It's a long process but if we weren't successful in 2008 there is no way he would have been able to hang on. But we were, and people started to realise that while there was new blood in the team the state of All Black rugby was really healthy.

Everyone loves jumping on the bandwagon when you win and when you lose everyone wants to get in there and give their opinion. But I hoped that they would give him another chance for at least another year. And then when all the Robbie versus Ted things started to happen I felt for him. I sent Ted a couple of texts and said that I was thinking about him and the other coaches, and when they finally got the job I texted him, 'Well done mate. It's bloody awesome news.' He texted back: 'Thanks for all your support.'

It was great, but you knew what Ted was going through. People were on his back. It even reached the stage where on the front of the paper it was reported that his house, which he had for sale, had dropped in value because of a landslide. His house was nowhere near where the landslip had happened. At our wedding we were talking to Raewyn and Ted, and Raewyn said how bad things had been for them, but now that Ted had been reappointed he was excited. He said to me when we were talking just after the ceremony, 'Look we are going to try and do this next year,' and I said to him, 'Ted, enjoy yourself mate, you know that rugby season is next year.' I got the impression that he was determined then and there to make things right.

Ted was hugely liked in the team and he had the backing of all the senior guys, and he didn't really need to be thinking about the way ahead so soon after his re-election. I thought it was great of the NZRU to give him another few years, even though they copped flak for the decision. It was actually a big step for our national psyche. It showed we had gone past the type of kneejerk reactions that had happened in the past. I think people tend to forget the stats about how the current coaching staff have been the most successful. People want to have someone to blame, to label them with being the reason we lost the World Cup. It is only a minority who think like that but they do make a lot of noise.

With that in mind, it was great that we were able to hang onto Smithy when it looked like he might leave after the 2008 Grand Slam tour. I heard he might be leaving when I was in Ireland. I didn't realise what was going on because of my later arrival on the tour. After the Irish test he congratulated me on my game. I put my arm around him and said, 'I've heard you are leaving.' And he said, 'Yeah, I'm thinking about it.' As players we talked to him about it. His biggest issue was being away from family a lot. Not so much when we were away as a team but he was doing a lot of work back in New Zealand, such as clinics for the High Performance Centre. So he'd be constantly away and obviously he was getting offered good money elsewhere too.

Smithy's a loyal sort of a guy. He would do anything for you and I know when he made a decision, it would have been the hardest decision he ever made. But I knew he made it for the guys around him that he loved. We didn't persuade him; we wanted him to know that he was *the* man. I think we forget sometimes as players that we've got to recognise that and we've got to acknowledge that to the coaches. They work so bloody hard and often don't appreciate how highly you think of them. I don't think Smithy realised that until we actually said it. We thought that he was the best in the business and if there was any way we could help him out in terms of maybe talking to someone or giving feedback then we would, and that's the way we went about it. He told us he had talked to his wife and was going to stay, so it was an awesome result.

I've got a lot of time for Smithy; he's done wonders for my game in terms of the way I think. I appreciate his faith in me as a player as well as his constructive criticism of my faults, which was why when I heard he might be leaving I made sure he knew what I thought about him. I said to him if there was anything I could do to help out I would. But I added that if he decided to go and if he had a contract for a fullback, I was available to go with him.

The other thing to come out of the World Cup was the change in Richie's captaincy. Obviously, we lost a core group of senior players after the World Cup so there was only a handful left. Richie really wanted to make sure we kept a grip on things. He would ask for feedback more often. He had different guys that he would talk to about on-field and off-field scenarios, and I think he was a different captain in 2008. He learnt a lot and was able to give more responsibility to others as opposed to taking everything on himself. You feel for Richie because he has a lot of things on his plate, not just the captaincy. There are the things that are not game related. He has a lot of off-field stuff that he has to put up with and in his position it is difficult to say no to things. He can't say no to people asking him about this or that, and we told him in 2008 that sometimes he had to force himself to say no. He needed to give some of his responsibilities to other guys so the load wasn't totally on his shoulders. He did that and he learnt from that. We were all thinking that we had to do really well in 2008. He was probably feeling that more than others because he was the skipper. He always leads by example in the way he plays and I think sharing the workload helped him immensely.

I don't know how he does it. He has to be top of his game the whole time and he is the top player in the world, with Dan Carter out there with him as well. But to be doing it year in and year out and be a captain at the same time is a massive responsibility. He not only has to think about his own game but the whole team and the way it goes as well. If I were to look back at the Richie in 2004 when we played Wales to the Richie we have now, he's a very different person. Now and then we talk about that game in Wales and we have a bit of a laugh about how he was the captain that year and just about lost his first game in the captaincy.

I've known Richie since we were school kids and I was playing against him. I think he's grown. His ability to be able to become the best, year in and year out, is just unbelievable. Add to that the pressure of his position. Invariably before games, especially overseas, all the media want to talk about is how Richie's cheating at the breakdown by doing this or doing that. It doesn't hold him back to be able to get in there and fight for the ball and still get turnovers and what not. You've got to have respect for someone who can do that. As far as I'm concerned he's a great captain.

Team-mates

Anton Oliver was around briefly in my first year in the All Blacks, in 2003. He got dropped before the Tri Nations and the World Cup. When you are a youngster going into teams you look to the guys who've been around a few years and he was always a top guy. I remember Rome in 2004 when he came back into the team and we all received our jerseys before playing Italy. The sheer emotion involved at reclaiming his jersey was obvious when he started bawling his eyes out. I was only starting to get into double figures in test appearances and when I saw that it was very moving. I didn't really know Anton that well, but I knew what he had been through.

At the same time it was hard to believe a guy like that, one of the hard men of the front row, was bawling his eyes out. But it was fair enough because he couldn't believe he'd be getting that jersey again. That's how special it was to him. Later on I read in his book what he went through at that moment. To me it showed how much you had to treasure your jersey.

It was fantastic having a guy like him in our team. Anton is really intelligent, he loved going away in his spare time and looking up information the way he did before giving his First World War presentation to us. Most guys would never want to do that stuff. There was one time we were in Paris and I bumped into him in the lift and asked what he was up to. He said he was going to an art exhibition and asked if I wanted to come along. I politely said, 'No, no thanks, you're all right.' And later on I thought, 'This guy's a geek.' But it was just him.

That war presentation he did was outstanding and it got us fired up. He also made a presentation on the Bledisloe Cup and what it all meant. Now that he's gone, Conrad Smith, being a lawyer, has taken on that role. It's nice to have that sort of attachment. I don't really know much about history. I certainly didn't know a lot of what went on before, and the fact that rugby played a part during the wars and how special that was to New Zealanders. You became more aware that it wasn't just about rugby, that there are a lot of things behind what we're doing, which is why New Zealanders are so attached to the All Blacks.

I've come through the grades with **Tony Woodcock**. He is a year younger than me. Those front rowers are all pretty dry. But Woody's quite a character and although he comes across as pretty dry sometimes, he's a good, decent bloke. Woody was always a quiet sort of guy. Occasionally, in his younger days, he would tag along with you. Nowadays, he has started to lead from the front, and that is especially the case since **Carl Hayman** left. As a result he is starting to get recognised a bit more. I don't think people realised he was an important part of what Carl could do back then. Woody's been around a long time as well. And certainly his technique, from what I hear — I don't know too much about what goes on in there — is certainly up there. And he's definitely got a long, long way to go in terms of his experience and how youthful he is.

Carl was similar to Woody in a lot of ways. These guys intrigue me; it's like they've got their own little club. Carl, Woody, Andrew Hore, and to a certain extent Kevey. They're always talking about hunting and fishing and drinking beer. And they get bloody damned good at doing that too.

Once we were in a team meeting and Wayne Smith was going around the room and asking 'What do we do here?' and 'How come this happened here?' He would stand up there — I'm sure Smithy knows it — and everyone tried to hide away and not make eye contact with him. I can't remember what the question was, but there was a dead silence in the room. It was one of those serious meetings, I think it was during the British Lions tour in 2005 so it was pretty stern stuff, and he picked on Carl. He asked Hayman the question, whatever it was. He just had a blank look on his face and everyone was thinking we were in trouble now. We were all going to suffer. But Zarg just replied, 'Oh, can I phone a friend?' His timing was perfect. It had all become pretty serious but the meeting just broke into hysterics. Even Smithy had to laugh. That was Carl Hayman. He'd come out with these random things every now and then, and his timing was always impeccable.

The way those front rowers worked on their roles made things a hell of a lot easier for the whole side. Back in 2004 when we were looking at where we needed to improve we decided that one of the most important things we had to get right was our set piece. When you saw those guys starting to destroy scrums and then having the strength to contribute in other areas, you couldn't help but have the greatest respect for them. When you're a prop, it is almost traditional for people to think you've got no skills and that sometimes they might get stuck out in the no-man's land of the backline. But in these situations our guys were so comfortable they were starting to call certain things, whether they were going to be sacrificial runners or things like that. That made things a whole lot easier for the backs. It used to be that for the majority of the time when you got a prop out there they would panic. You could have passed them the ball and they wouldn't have known what they were going to do with it. However, these guys knew instantly what to do if they got stuck out there. They were really smart about how they could use themselves effectively, without disrupting some of the back play, which was outstanding.

I think there's a big difference between our front rowers and those in the northern hemisphere and, to some extent, the Australians and the South Africans. We can mix it up with the physical stuff but we've also got good ball carriers who can pass effectively. The way someone like **Keven Mealamu** plays is amazing. When we're playing our conditioning games he's basically another back. He's chipping the ball and he's always got this grubber that he does out of nowhere. He catches the ball, grubbers to himself and collects it, nine times out of 10. I don't think you see many other guys around the world do that. Maybe it's the way we are over here and the way we play. We've got a bit more flair than perhaps just hitting rucks and mauls and scrummaging and lifting in lineouts. Our tight five certainly are more dynamic.

Ali Williams is one person who really expresses himself and who is not afraid to try things, even with kicking. He'll call certain things, and if you gave him the opportunity to kick goals he would do it. Again I think it's the mentality we have. I suppose as kids it is about picking up the rugby ball and having a go. There's not too much of that narrow-minded thinking that 'I'm a forward, I've just got to hit rucks'. I think we've got that different aspect to our development. Ali's always been his own person. He doesn't often think about what he's going to say before he says it, and that's just the way he is. You wouldn't change that. He is quite bubbly and cheeky in a unique way. In a team situation he's probably not far off what he comes across as on the field or the way he comes off in public. He's probably a little more outgoing with us, but apart from that what you see is what you get with Ali. He's out there and loves to use his voice in certain ways and is not one to shy off talking about things.

You can always tell when the locks are up against a formidable opponent, say a Victor Matfield. You see that extra intensity in the way they train. They'll call more meetings to go through their lineouts and what they're going to call, and do a full analysis of what they're going to do to win more lineouts. It's not only against Victor and the South Africans but also the Australians, because these guys know that they're up against the world's best. Why wouldn't you want to be on your game? The South Africans and Australians can be formidable, especially when they win their lineouts cleanly and start to drive. The South Africans love to drive as often as they can. That's probably the hardest thing for the forwards to handle.

Keith Robinson was a hard man. He wore his heart on his sleeve in certain ways. He loved getting stuck in and starting stuff. I don't think he liked being classed as a hard man. I think that image developed because of the way he went about his game. It was the way people saw it. And you'd say to him, 'Oh yeah, the hard man,' and he'd blush about it.

Towards the end of his career he was starting to come right physically after some terrible injury problems. I had a few talks with Robbo here and there about the injuries he was going through and what he was battling with to try to stay on the field. The effort he made was pretty outstanding, especially considering coming back again after such a lengthy injury. That

177

spoke volumes about how determined he was. Not only did he go away and keep working to get through pain barriers, but he became an All Black again. Robbo was quite a shy guy who did his talking on the field. Everything he did, even at training, was done at 100 per cent. Sometimes when we did contact sessions, guys would be a bit light-hearted. But you never got that with Robbo. A few guys used to get upset that they went into a ruck a bit lightly and then found Robbo flying through trying to waste them. That was his way. If he was going to be around, you made sure you braced yourself and you weren't going in half-hearted, because he definitely wouldn't be.

Chris Jack was great in the team. His responsibility was to look after the new guys coming in and show them the way. Off the field he had meetings with the younger players just to let them know how things worked. He was a very unselfish guy, and a hard worker. I found those Canterbury guys were like that. They're team-mate first and foremost. They didn't want to let their team-mate down, and were selfless about their time. Jacko was one of those guys. All the Canterbury guys enjoyed their rugby. As the years went on and I got to know him a bit better, we joked around a little more and shared ideas, and a couple of times I went in and sat in on his meetings. He'd almost be that sort of older cousin the new guys would look up to and listen to. He did things subtly to make them feel at ease. He instantly made them feel welcomed to the All Blacks, whereas a few years before it was almost a daunting thing to come into the side.

Brad Thorn is a good man. I've played a couple of seasons with him now, in 2003 and 2008. He's a hard man; he loves the physical side. It's amazing that you see what you see in the league terms, and you think he's one of those guys who loves to get in there and have a bit of biff. I don't know about biff or anything, but he does love getting among the hard stuff. He's got that croaky voice, which he says is from all the high tackles in league.

I think it's amazing how he transformed his game from league to rugby. I had a talk with him in 2008 about how he'd kept himself going for so long because he had an awesome year at the age of 33. He said that the year he took off when he was 27 was the best decision he made. He went away and did a bit of labouring and took that whole year to freshen up. Then one day he looked in the mirror and said, 'It's time to get back into it.' He's got a wicked sense of humour, Thorny, because he always goes on about it when you're watching league. If we are watching a State of Origin game, all you hear from the room is him yelling stuff out like, 'Get that into you, get that into you,' as big shots were being given to someone. There're certain people who love promoting themselves and showing off different parts of their bodies. He says he just does it for a laugh but he'll come up behind me and say, 'Oh yeah, your chest is pretty big, I'll put you in the top six in the team,' and you're quietly chuffed about that. And then he says, 'Oh, that's after Conrad,' obviously knowing that Conrad hasn't got too much on him. It's those sorts of things he keeps on about. I'm sure he only does it to me, I don't know why. Of course you give it back to him and he's a really good-natured man.

It's amazing the way things have turned out for **Richie McCaw**. Through the grades Josh Blackie was in front of him and Richie was always on the bench, or thereabouts. But to see him come on in leaps and bounds was great because you always knew how good he was. Josh Kronfeld was leading the way back then. Richie did things similar to what Kronfeld did, but in time Richie has taken open-side play to a different level, I think. Not only did he get in there and disrupt ball, but he was stealing ball, and he was doing it all the time.

There are some players you look at and see their physiques and you think, 'Man, he's going to be awesome.' Richie's not overly muscular, but he's hard. That's probably why he never gets moved when he goes into those rucks; he's always there. And he's really intelligent about how he goes about it.

His captaincy has changed. I think to start with, he always considered he needed to talk a lot. And I suppose as a captain that's probably something I came across when I first captained the Chiefs in 2008. You think you've always got to be the voice all the time. I look back at that and realise he's changed his leadership and the way that he gets his message across via other voices. That's a great gift to have. To be well respected in what you do on the field, and to have the sense to be able to voice your leadership through other guys and share your workload, shows great skill. Because the last thing you want, as a player, is to hear the same voice, the same old thing, all the time.

Richie's taken his leadership to new heights, and all the time he has to cope with claims that he is cheating. When you're playing against him you always think that, and you always think the ref is going to be on it. Despite that, he still seems to get in there and do it. He's obviously doing it legally because no matter how many people have analysed him, he carries on. Occasionally he'll show you a couple of his techniques when you're at training and how we can maybe get a bit lower to get in there and claim the ball. But I don't know how a guy like him can get around and do that so often. It would be a good question to ask a lot of the other flankers around New Zealand, or around the world, because Richie took the game to a new level by getting in there and stealing a lot of the ball.

If I was in his shoes, being talked about like that in match after match would affect my game. I think there are probably times when he hears a couple of things here and there and he just chuckles. It makes him go in even harder. He doesn't show any doubts he might be feeling or concerns that the refs might be watching him closely. It doesn't faze him at all. That's why he's one of the best rugby players New Zealand's ever seen.

Marty Holah was very talented. He was loved in the Waikato and what he did for Waikato and the All Blacks was awesome. But I think he'd be the first to say that he was probably a little bit behind Richie, as a lot of guys are. But he was a grafter and a hard man who loved to get among it. And, unfortunately, Richie was coming through and starting to really stamp his mark on world rugby. Marty was probably getting on a little bit, and not quite as tall as Richie. But he was a top team man. I had a lot of time for Marty; he was a really decent bloke and down to earth, just a humble guy, and I admired him.

Jerry Collins always spoke his mind and, with JC, you know he actually goes away and thinks about what he says. I'm sure some of the things he came up with in the media were the result of that. JC is another guy who came through the grades with me. He didn't mind saying what he believed and I suppose that's always been his attitude. He didn't care what other people thought about what he said. I suppose when he was brought up in Porirua it probably helped that he could back it up with his fists as well. He was a hard man, he had to be to play again after his bad injury. What I also admired in JC in the latter part of his All Black career was the way he changed his game. Four, five or six years ago you knew that when JC got the ball, all he was going to do was run straight, drop his shoulder and try to get into you. And if you ran it back there was always that bloody arm waiting to give you one. But he changed his game. He ran it back hard and all of sudden we started to see these wee short balls he popped to other guys. He looked at his game and the changes probably came from rugby league. He got on well with Gordon Tallis.

Jerry's a great guy off the field. I had a lot of time with him and laughed heaps and joked around with him. Being in the same age group helped. We always liked to talk, and some of the Samoan boys used to give each other stick in Samoan. But, at the same time, he was also his own man. He'd go up to the pub by himself and you'd be walking along and there was JC coming out of the TAB or pub, and you would ask what he'd been up to and he'd say, 'I just went down to have a pint.'

I thought he retired from the All Blacks too soon. He had an awesome World Cup. But there are times in Super rugby when you start to see little things about the body language of your mates, the way they go about things and you know they are uninterested. I saw that in Jerry's game in 2008. He also wasn't the bubbly JC I knew. I still thought he left a bit early, but you knew what his mindset was. As it turned out, it was probably the best thing he's done. He would have thought long and hard about it and obviously it's showed in the way he played before he left. It's always sad to see a player go overseas, especially as he's certainly a decent guy and one of your mates, but you know he's going to go on to brighter things and hopefully he enjoys it over there. JC's the type of person who once he's made a decision he goes about doing it. If it's not the right one, he'll just stick at it and make another decision and then stick at it again.

Rodney So'oialo is a family guy, like Kevey, who wants to go out there and play some really hard footy. Occasionally we'd talk about Titch and the Sevens years and the Colts years we shared. He and Kevey are similar guys and that's probably why they still hang around together a lot. They are hard cases when on the golf course. Normally, when there are just two of you, you cheat a little bit. You both know you are doing it. But when Rodney hits a ball he'll say, 'Oh, nah nah, I don't think it should be there, I should move it back into a rougher spot.' And Kevey will go, 'No, that's all right, mate, just put it a little bit closer.' But that's the way these guys are, they're honest and family-orientated sorts of guys.

I take my hat off to them. They've got kids and they've traveled away on and off for a long period. I only went through that pull in the latter part of 2008. I better understood what those guys and other fathers went through when away from their families for that long. It's something you don't appreciate until you go through it yourself. They don't walk around moping about their families, but I know I did in the last two weeks of that 2008 tour. They have been doing it every year, year in and year out. They must miss their families to bits. And now I understand why they buy all those presents. They always go out shopping together, especially in Paris, and they come back with special gifts for their families. But you certainly realise why your partner and your kids deserve it when you're away that long.

Rod went through a patch in 2004–05 when he was heavily criticised, then came back the following year and won the player of the year award. That was testimony to his approach because that criticism would have hurt. It's awesome to come through with a guy like Rodney as well, especially with a New Zealand Sevens background, to be able to push on through and become All Blacks. Back when we were in the Sevens we enjoyed wearing that black jersey, but we always had the dream of becoming a full All Black without ever thinking we were going to make it. Rod understood all we'd gone through with Titch.

Justin Marshall was a bit like Anton, he'd been round a hell of a long time. I didn't have too much to do with him. Marshie was still a little bit old school, which meant he didn't talk to young guys. But he was decent enough. He was competitive in every respect. He drove things hard, but on the other side of it he could be a bloody sook too. He could sulk about different things. You didn't want to upset him in any way because you know he'd be bitter about it. Mind you, most halfbacks are probably like that. If he didn't win or he didn't like something, he could get pretty sour about it.

We had the connection of being from Southland and him from Mataura. In my younger days we knew all about Justin Marshall and how he had moved to Canterbury. But when you see a player like him when you're in Invercargill you always call them Southlanders. Simon Forrest did the same thing. So it was great to be able to play in the same team as Marshie because he was also the most capped back as well. I remember back in 2003 at my first World Cup, we were having a few drinks after a pool game, and he said, 'Everyone stand up. Sit down if this is your first World Cup.' And a lot of guys sat down. 'Your second' and another group sat down. And he said, 'Your third?' And he was probably the only one left standing. I don't know why he did that at all. But I do remember thinking, 'He's been to three World Cups, how the heck can this guy still be going?' That made a big impression on me. It was great to see that experience and to know he could still mix it with the best in the world as a halfback.

Byron Kelleher was quite a contrast to Marshie. In some ways he didn't think about what he said before he said it. He was definitely a guy who wore his heart on his sleeve. He put his all into everything. And perhaps he overdid it because he cared so much about people and was so passionate about things. He probably didn't have balance. He was like a Coke can that had been shaken and when you opened it, it was all fizzed up. He was like that 24/7, not just before the game or in the game, he was full on like that all the blooming time.

Although he was ultra-competitive, he cared about what he believed in and all the small things in life, and also about his team-mates. For a long time he sat on that bloody length of pine and never got games. But he was always there to help out Marshie. You could imagine if you sat for as long as he did how much you'd want to move on. But he was very unselfish, and he got his reward in the end by being able to start so many games.

Byron loved life off the field. He loved getting into sort of celebrity status and making sure he was getting invites to the best nightclubs. He wasn't afraid to ring up people and say, 'Hey look, I'm Byron Kelleher, I'm with the All Blacks. Can you sort something out here for us?' He would say we needed a cordoned off area in a club. The guys mocked him about doing that, because none of us would dream of doing it. But we loved it when he sorted it out. It was funny one time when we were in Ireland. He rang up a club and did his usual and said we would love to come to the club. And the guy at the other end said, 'Yeah, whatever,' and hung up. Then he rang back and he said, 'No, it's Byron Kelleher, I'm with the All Blacks, is there a place where we can come and can you cordon off an area for us?' The club guy still didn't buy it. I think he had to ring up three or four times, and by then the guy believed him. It takes balls to be able to do something like that, not just to do it once but the number of times he did. He was great at organising things for the guys to do. He was there for the team first.

Now **Brendan Leonard** has emerged. Harry's a great football player. He's a quieter type of guy who has got a massive future. He had a wee setback in 2008 with injury. But to see the way he's come through from being in the wider training group then onto the Waikato bench and then getting his opportunity is great. And he took it with both hands. You would have thought he'd been round a few more years than he has, but his game is on the rise. He's going to be awesome. And he's great for us in Waikato and the Chiefs. He's a halfy with a really good pass, he gets around, loves to snipe around the blind and around the rucks, and he's got out and out pace. With his left foot he gets a lot of height in his box kicks, and he's starting to lead. Like most players he was really conservative when he first came in, and he didn't want to talk. But now he's starting to come up with his own ideas. The way he plays the game I'm sure he'll be in the black jersey for a long time.

Piri Weepu is a little different as a halfback. In some ways Pow doesn't look like an athlete but he is very powerful, he loves running with the ball, his passing is right up there and he can also play two positions. He's talented. He's almost like a leaguey in the way he plays the game, which is why he always talks about league, and also about touch rugby.

Pow needs to keep going to find what's good for him. I believe he's going through a stage at the moment where he's working out the things that make him tick. When you saw the way he led that Wellington team in 2008 and the way he played with that extra responsibility, it was great. It's funny how often players respond under those circumstances. He's definitely one who responds the greater the expectations are of him. If Pow can keep that up, he can mix it at the top end for a long time.

Andy Ellis has been there for a while now, and **Jimmy Cowan**. Two years ago Jimmy started to knock on the door. Once he took care of his off-field antics, where he clearly needed a hand, he had the sense to realise how fortunate he was that the Rugby Union gave him another chance. You don't get that very often, but it served to wake him up and his response was positive, because it doesn't always happen like that. And then a bit of luck went Jimmy's way when Andy was injured. Sometimes that is all you need. Someone's misfortune was his good luck and he only needed a sniff to get out there. I suppose he had something to prove as well, not to us as players or to the management, but to the public.

I roomed with him in Dunedin the week after the Wellington test against South Africa in 2008. We had travelled to Wellington Airport together and he looked tired, or worried, about something. I looked at him and started laughing then said: 'Hey mate, are you all right?' And he told me he had been involved in an incident. I told him not to tell me any more and that he didn't have to worry about me saying anything. We all know what came of that. But once it was dealt with he was really up to play. But he didn't get onto the field in that game. For that whole week he was pumped and couldn't wait to get out there. What that told me was that he was keen to get out there and prove himself.

We all know what a good year we had. Jimmy played an outstanding game when we beat Australia on Eden Park. His performance was a key part of us winning that night. Then being given the captaincy of the Highlanders meant he had some extra pressure, and that's perhaps all he needed. He's grown up and moved on from that phase in his life. It's hard because people don't realise that these guys are still in their mid-20s and they want to go out there and enjoy themselves like everyone else. It's hard when you see your mates having fun and not often having to suffer the consequences of what they do.

We all know different mates who do things they shouldn't. But they don't get published in papers. And that's especially the case when you come from Mataura. All your mates are around you and you don't want to be seen as a superstar who doesn't go out and have a drink. There is peer pressure you have to deal with. It's hard to make decent decisions and not realise the consequences if you do stuff up when you're that young.

And it's funny, it only takes something like that to make you realise that you've got to make sure you're respectable in front of the public. You are in some way public property. The other side of that is when you have had to learn the hard way. But once you've come through the hard times and then got it sorted, it is a great feeling. Obviously, Jimmy would love to have avoided what happened but he probably wouldn't change it because if you learn from it you are stronger, which he showed by coming back and challenging for the No. 9 spot.

I've already said what a relaxed sort of guy **Dan Carter** is. He is now starting to run the team and letting us know how he likes things done. Never in your wildest dreams would you believe how laid-back DC is, especially now he is in a pressure cooker position every time he plays. A lot of guys would fold under that heat but not him. He's instrumental in the way that we go about our game plans and the way we play the game. He's an impeccable part of the All Black team and also New Zealand rugby. You can see that because he's all the kids talk about. They want to be Dan Carters. There'll be right-foot kickers who want to be left-foot kickers now. All of a sudden you're seeing all these left-footed kickers coming through. So, it's great for New Zealand.

I've got a lot of time for **Stephen Donald**. He's an outgoing young man in a crucial position and I have been lucky to see him become an All Black from the Chiefs and Waikato teams. What he has achieved is outstanding and he had a fine year in 2008. One of his faults is that he lets other people's thoughts and criticism get to him. If he can learn to back himself, he can be an All Black for a long time. He has an unorthodox running and kicking style, but I have seen the work he has put into that side of the game. It is vital that guys like Stephen, Richard Kahui and Kevin O'Neill stick around for the Chiefs. Teams like the Crusaders have their Reuben Thornes and Justin Marshalls who sometimes won't get a start for their side but who set the standards for the younger guys both on and off the field. Stephen, Richard and Kevin are still young but they will be a crucial part of the Chiefs' future. Stephen is a great team man and on the odd Sunday we have enjoyed a few quiet beers talking about a few things and he is a guy who cares about all his team-mates and for that he is well respected in the Waikato.

Aaron Mauger, **Luke McAlister** and **Ma'a Nonu** are three quite different second-fives. Aaron had the ability to see the game and I believe he will make a very good coach. He was just so on to it with what he could see in a game and how a game worked and how it all unfolded. He could visualise the different strategies and had an ability to read how we could make things better. Like JC, he spoke his mind. He wasn't afraid to say that an idea the coach had brought up didn't sound too good. It's pretty hard to do something like that; I know I find that difficult. Not only do you have to know it's not right, but you have to put it in a way that's not offending them. They are your coaches and you don't want to get dropped for speaking out. Aaron was really good at stuff like that. He'd been around a while with the All Blacks and tactically he was very sound.

Luke's come on a bit. At the World Cup he was one of those players who had started to blossom. He's done well overseas and it's good news that he's coming back. It's pretty hard when you're going that well over there and he's obviously enjoying it. But he's very talented, he can kick goals, he's got flair and the ability to be able to run the ball, and with those massive thighs he can definitely break the game open. I've had a couple of seasons with Luke and he's starting to mature and become more of a leader in teams and in the way they play the game. Lukey loves having a go, running the ball back and tucking it under his arm and really having a decent crack, which is probably similar to Ma'a Nonu's style.

Ma'a did that in his early days, no matter what happened. If there was a three-man overlap he would charge ahead, because he wanted to run, to express himself. He's come a long way. He was criticised for the way he played, people asked whether he could tackle, if he could kick, why he didn't pass, why he could be so inconsistent. He probably took some time to find his position and have someone backing him the way the coaches have supported him. He's always been Ma'a; from the first time he was named in the All Blacks he was always going to be a very talented footballer and he needed to find a position he wanted to play. And it's hard when you can play so many positions. It certainly would have been tough for Ma'a. One minute he was playing on the wing the whole time, and he had an awesome Super 14 in 2008, but then all of a sudden he was thrown into the test side at second five. I don't know where his mind was at then but to snap out of it like he did showed how good he is.

By the end of 2008 he was right up there in terms of the players of the year. He had found consistency in his game. Running off Ma'a is one of the best things you can do, because you always know he's going to at least draw one, if not two, defenders, and slip the ball to you. Some of the criticism was that he can't kick, but he can. He hasn't been given that opportunity. At every training session he'll do it. He's a very skilful guy. But a lot of people don't see that in him because of the way he runs.

Ma'a off the field is one of the clowns of the team. He always has a new saying every time he comes into the team. You can guarantee that whether it is something as simple as 'Sorry about that' or some of the slang he comes up with, you will be talking that way yourself when you get home. I'd be away for a month or so and go home, and be practically talking a different language. That's the sort of thing he is responsible for. He's the one guy you don't want to get into a teasing sort of an argument with, because he always wins. He's got the gift of the gab and loves trashing people that way. He's a good storyteller and the sort of character you need to have on a team. He'd be one of the funniest guys I've been with in the team.

Conrad Smith was one player I played against in our early days. Snake's a very intelligent player and quite consistent. People think there's not much on him but the way he tackles and turns up in the right place at the right time makes him an invaluable player. He's had a few years to sit behind Tana and learn. There's also been a lot of competition in the centres with the likes of Ma'a coming through and that has been helpful for him. Conrad is very sound and has real ability in reading the game. That has been important because in the last few years the position of centre has changed so much, something I can appreciate from my own experience. But, like Ma'a, Conrad has put his hand up again. In 2008 he was carrying an injury yet was still consistent and solid in all he did. He didn't do anything flash but he was a guy you could rely on to tackle or to put into a space. And that's what you want from a centre, a guy who's going to put you into space and make sure he doesn't let the bigger centres through. He plays a big role off the field for the All Blacks with the social and music committees.

Richard Kahui, on the other hand, loves getting among the action. He enjoys making the hits, getting out of the defence system to make that spot hit and the blindside hit he loves. He thrives in the Waikato set-up, the blitz defence. When I first joined the Chiefs he was in the wider training group and I wondered why he was there and not in the main squad. Then he went to Otago and joined the Highlanders where he shone. Now, as he has come though, he's shown he has the ability to pass the ball.

He's a good guy off the field and he lives around the corner from me, so we catch up for a beer now and then. He's starting to bring solidity to his game. The experience he had in the All Blacks in 2008 helped him. He's starting to see the game now. He's starting to think about the bigger picture as opposed to the thought, 'I'll just make a couple of big hits and make a couple of big runs and that's it.' As a centre, you've got to start thinking about your outsides and putting them away.

He's learning about consistency too. In Super 14 you can have an odd game where you might not play well, because you've always got the next week to try to fix it. But with the All Blacks, and in international play, you might not be picked for the following week. So, I think he and Stephen Donald learnt a hell of a lot from being in that All Black camp. There is a rub-off there for the Chiefs as well, with more All Blacks in the squad. For a while it was just me, Sitiveni and Sione Lauaki who had been in there. We always tried to share different things we had learned, but the Chiefs and Waikato players still couldn't see the picture. Siti and I would share things with the others but Richard and Stephen would disagree with us at times. But it's worked out all right now, because they see what we're talking about, which hopefully will be reflected in the Chiefs and for Waikato.

I've already mentioned what **Doug Howlett** did for my career in the early days and what I learnt off him, and what a fantastic player he has been.

Joe Rokocoko was pretty raw when he became an All Black. I suppose the fact that he made Super 14 and the Blues won it in 2003 helped him. He hadn't played any Air New Zealand Cup, or NPC as it was back then, and we both made it into the All Blacks that year. Almost immediately

Chris Latham (left) of the Reds was a fullback I rated very highly. The Chiefs took this 2006 Super 14 encounter 35–17.

It was always nice getting away from Bryan Habana for a try against South Africa. We won this test in Pretoria 45–26.

Conflicting emotions at the 2007 Rugby World Cup. Delight (above) in diving for a try in our opener against Italy in Marseille, but disappointment (below) when giving my boots away to fans at our hotel at the Vale, outside Cardiff, after our quarter-final loss to France.

On the break at Eden Park in our 39–10 turnaround win over Australia in the 2008 Tri Nations series.

Taking in the sights of Dublin with Isaia Toeava on the 2008 Grand Slam tour.

Teaching the boys, Piri Weepu and Ma'a Nonu, how to play cards on the train to Limerick.

Meeting up with my father Fagalulu.

Our wedding day. Pictured, from left: Brother Danny holding nephew Mika, sister Victoria, Mum Ita, grandmother Alofa, Hayley, me, grandfather Lemana, stepfather Lia-Runi, brother Runi, brother Alesana, brother Faolua and Dad Fagalulu.

Hayley and me on our wedding day in 2007.

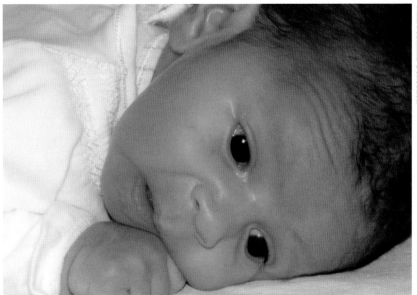

Max Muliaina arrives, and (bottom) Max after his hole-in-the-heart operation, which was a great success.

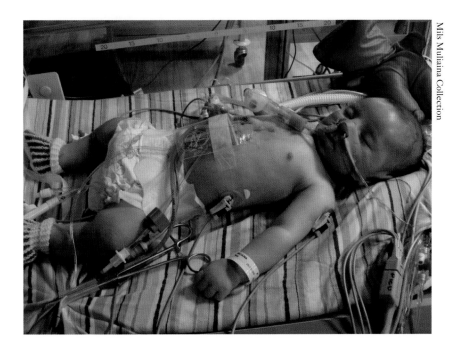

Max Muliaina and his proud Dad after Max had recovered from his heart surgery.

he was straight into it. The Rocket Man, he was scoring from everywhere, with his sheer pace and ability to change pace and work hard. Roks always wants to learn, he's always asking questions — what can I do here, and what happens there? When he's really sure on something, watch out. But if Joe's unsure then things might not go too well.

I always remember in 2003 when we played the Hurricanes. We won the game but at one stage we gave the ball to Joe and he had it on Tana, but you could almost see him thinking, 'Oh, that's Tana; there's no way I'll get round him.' He would definitely have scored, but he passed the ball and it was fumbled into touch. I've faced that situation myself, but not so close to the goal-line. When Joe was dead certain, he would go for it, which was why he scored so many tries. It was nice to see him back on the Grand Slam tour in 2008 after he got over his hand injury. It took its toll on him. A few years ago he was dropped by the Blues and that was pretty tough for him to take. I sent him a text at the time telling him to keep his head up. Generally, he's the sort of guy who can see positives in most things.

Sitiveni Sivivatu in my view is the probably the most intelligent Fijian I have ever met in terms of his rugby analysis. He is so smart in knowing the tactical things and how to manipulate teams and what we can do in different places. The problem is with the language difficulty he doesn't know how to explain it. It's not until you're sitting out on the field or standing out there and talking one on one that you get what he means. He's got an ability to read play, and to also come up with different ideas. That's why I think he is probably the smartest wing I've known. It shows when he gets into that first receiver role. He is very dangerous there. You could think he was just moping around but then, all of a sudden, he'll go. If you show a little bit of ball movement he's away, or he'll put someone into space.

Sometimes he's a bit lazy, and you know when Siti's not in the right frame of mind. Occasionally at the start of a campaign he turns up and the belly's looking a little bit big and the kick chase isn't as hard as what it usually is. You know you've got to give him a little bit more time and still keep in his ear encouraging him. You tell him, 'Mate, it's all right, it's fine, just keep on doing what you're doing.' Because he'll certainly create more chances than not, and that's what you want from him.

I rate him highly among the wingers round the world. I think he had a quiet year in 2008 and I think he's pretty determined to do well in 2009. But Siti was solid. He did all the good things you want him to do, he worked hard and did the things off the ball. A lot of the criticism he had in 2008 was because people didn't see the flashy stuff he's so good at doing, but they overlooked some of the hard work that he did opening up spaces for players. People are constantly looking at the ball and they don't see how hard some of the wings work, and he's one of them. That's the way things are, really — people are so concentrated on what's going on with the big thing and a lot of the time the flashy things look a lot better than the harder stuff.

Grand Slam
Diary 2008

Sunday, 26 October

All Blacks team named. Excited at thought of being in team, it's always a great feeling — but is fair to say I had Hayley's pregnancy heavily on my mind. The team is due to leave tomorrow and with Hayley being two days' overdue now it was looking as if I was going to miss the Monday 11.55 pm departure with the team. Assembled with the team for outfitting, and had a meeting with the coaches and captain's group to discuss the next campaign. Hayley and Mum (up for the birth) have travelled to Auckland with me and are staying in another hotel close by just in case, and because we are seeing the specialist on Monday morning again about the baby.

Monday, 27 October

I have missed the gym session with the team this morning as our appointment is at Middlemore Hospital at 9 am. Specialist has decided to induce today, which came as a complete surprise. Thinking it's all on now, have rung team doctor Debs [Robinson] to inform her of the news — as am meant to train with team this arvo and we have team photos. Induction process is started, leaving with team looking unlikely — however, we have Plan B in place with management that I can catch the Tuesday flight and arrive in Hong Kong Wednesday morning.

Tuesday, 28 October

It has been a long night trying to sleep on a Lazyboy in Hayley's birthing room. The induction by injection was not working so we are now trying a drip. At about 1 pm we finally have some action. I thought the adrenalin and excitement of a test match was up there, but my lack of sleep is overtaken by pure adrenalin. At 2.10 pm Wow, Wow, Wow — I cannot believe I have experienced this. It has to be the best moment of my life. Max Muliaina was born, 9.6 pounds. The jubilation was shared with family, friends and team-mates by text. I have been telling Hayley I would not send a text announcement as I thought they were geeky, but I couldn't control the delight I felt inside and wanted to share it with those people closest to us. It read 'Finally Max Muliaina has arrived weighing in at 9.6 pounds!' I must say Hayley has done a magnificent job and I have so much respect for women who have gone through not only carrying a child for nine months but the delivery — man, that in itself is something amazing. I have spoken to Ted and informed him I would still like to travel but not till Wednesday, which would mean I would arrive in Hong Kong on Thursday. I was then named to start the test.

Wednesday, 29 October

Due to leave later tonight. But six hours before departure Max is having a few complications and is breathing too fast and is struggling to breast feed. Hayley broke down for the third time and the thought of something going wrong while I was away — I could never forgive myself. I have always said family will come first and although there was a burning desire to play in Hong Kong this was truly a time to put my son and family before rugby. Phoned Ted and he was completely supportive of my decision. I stressed my point that I was sorry to let him down but he was quick to say that that was not the case at all and I needed to put my family first.

Thursday, 30 October

Specialist has seen Max and he is doing okay — think the little toad just didn't want me to go. Thought I'd better keep on the training side so went over to the Domain (Hayley and Max now at Birth Care opposite the Domain). Looking back now I think I made a great decision — in hindsight I would have arrived Thursday two days before a game with lack of sleep and my mind elsewhere. I would not have done the All Blacks jersey the justice it deserves.

Friday, 31 October

Did a gym session to keep the body ticking over. I have had a lot of congratulations from the public as Max's arrival has been announced in the papers and on TV. Not too sure how the news got out but apparently I phoned Ted during the middle of a press conference!

Saturday, 1 November

Finally at home. Hard watching the game. I found myself texting Ice to wish him all the best and tell him he had the goods to play and concentrate on the basics. He had a great game. I am so delighted for him as a lot of people have been on his back in the last few years — he got Player of the Day.

Sunday, 2 November

Nappies, bottles and repeat, over and over again . . .

Monday, 3 November

Training in morning, a very hard session as I know I have to train a lot harder as I haven't played a game since the Barbarians — and the desire to get my jersey back still burns inside me. I must admit a little bit inside me is fearful of losing that jersey, but I can't let that control my thoughts. I just have to do this and work myself as hard as I can to know and have peace of mind so that when I go into the team environment I am at their level, or close to it, as opposed to being a few weeks behind. Mum has gone back to Invercargill. Always sad to see my mum leave as being so far away I never get to see my family as much as I would like to.

Tuesday, 4 November

Gym in the morning as I have lost a lot of weight during the course of Hayley's labour — I struggle to keep my weight on at the best of times and have dropped 3 kilos.

Wednesday, 5 November

Have a couple of outings with Max — have trained and put my body through one of the hardest workouts of the last two weeks. Counting down now the days till I jump on the plane — as I leave on Friday to join the team. Now all of a sudden Max is restless and won't sleep in his bassinet. The only place he likes is his dad's arms. Are kids really that smart? Unfortunately, this time Max it's not going to work and I have to get going.

Saturday, 8 November, 12.17 pm (NZ time):
Transit Hong Kong Airport

Well, have left home, things have been really busy over the last two days, Max's breathing got worse so we paid a visit to Carol (midwife) in Auckland. Two hours later the little man was admitted into Starship Hospital. He has a hole in his heart, not sure the exact name of it but all in all very scary moment for myself and Hayley, given the fact it's our first child and I was due to leave the next day. Hayley, of course, was in a terrible state, I rang the doc and informed her of the news and that I would let them know what I was going to do. Very difficult decision. My first, sorry, our first child, and having to decide whether to pull out of the tour. My conversation with Debs was at 11.30 am and I was taking off at 11.55 pm that night. She just said that I needed to do what was right for myself, who and why I'm going on tour for.

To cut a long story short, the doctors thought that Max was doing well and that this operation happens a lot so they would look to do it in three or so weeks. Hayley and I, and her sister, thought it best if I went overseas. I mean in which normal profession would they let you have four weeks off? The coaches have been outstanding and very supportive. Ted just needed to know either way so they could plan who to replace me with, but he said to do what was right for me and my family. So here I am in transit in Hong Kong after the bumpiest ride ever. I'm heading to London and am due to arrive Saturday afternoon of the Scotland Test. I will stay the night in London and then meet up with the team on the flight to Dublin. I have just had a text from Ma'a to remind me to bring his dreads that he had sent to my house. Arrive in London, have to take express train feeling very stressed out as normally bus and everything is organised and I'm used to following someone with the same tracksuit on. Find my way there safe and sound, had a stretch and met Tony Hanks for a drink, dinner and a pub to watch the game on TV. Went to Wagamama for dinner. Have not watched a game in a pub since 2000. Missed first half due to it being a soccer mad city and couldn't find a pub playing the rugby.

Sunday, 9 November

Sunday morning in London. I tried to shake some of the cobwebs from my flight by going for a run through Hyde Park. After breakfast I took a stroll looking for an electronics shop so I could buy the necessary equipment to make Skype calls back home. Had a coffee at Starbucks while contemplating catching up with the team. I am excited to be joining up with them again. The doc texted me last night to let me know about Isaia and what the dress call would be for today. I rang New Zealand and talked to Mum and also Hayley. It was funny waking up this morning as I felt I would have to be changing nappies. I have certainly felt the change in temperature and have the heating turned up which makes me feel flu-ish. But I am feeling good and ready for action.

I caught up with the team when they arrived at Heathrow. I had made sure I was there in plenty of time, four hours early in fact. We then boarded our flight to Dublin, but just as they were backing it out it developed engine problems and they had to be attended to, which took about an hour. We arrived in Dublin at 9.30 in the evening.

Monday, 10 November

It was straight into touring routine today. At 10 am we had a strategy meeting, then at 10.30 am there was a team meeting. At 11 am the training team was named. It feels great to be back among the boys and enjoying lots of laughs. We had a media session after training and I had to face plenty of questioning about Max as a result of joining the team late but that all went fine. The team had a pool recovery session for those who had played against Scotland. And there was also time for some gym work. The laundry call was made. This can be one of the most important requirements on the tour. You are given a time by which you need to have your laundry ready and you need to be there with it on time or you have to wait until another day to get it done.

This is especially important if you want to have your training gear laundered so you can use it the next day. I also picked up some thermals to wear from equipment manager Errol Collins. For a long time I didn't wear thermals and almost became superstitious about wearing them because I thought I might not play so well. I never felt comfortable in them. But I have started to use them more this year and it is quite cold so they will be useful.

Being back among the team it was good to be relaxing in the team room. This is like a nerve centre in our accommodation in every location. It is where our laptops are set up. There is sometimes a table tennis table and there are fridges with supplies of water and Powerade. Usually there's a big screen TV where we can watch DVDs. A treatment table is usually there as well, and some food will generally be available. There's always someone in there and it is where we get notices about our dress codes for the next day or so and our schedules.

Speaking of food, it is good to be eating properly again. Back at the hospital we had been getting only a couple of meals a day but with the team it was the full nutritional deal at the required times of the day. In the afternoon the backs had a meeting about our defence, our goals for the Ireland test and our opportunities for the game.

Tuesday, 11 November

Early today we had a team meeting about our opportunities and our defence for the game but training was disappointing, mainly because of the poor field we had to practise on. Afterwards we had a pool session with the hot and cold treatments. Richie let me know that Smithy was thinking about leaving. That was disappointing because as far as I am concerned Smithy has been the best backs coach of all time for me. It was bad enough that Mick Byrne was leaving for Japan. He has done so much for my game and been an awesome help. We had a visit to the Guinness Brewery later and had dinner there which was great. It is an awesome place to visit. They gave us each a present of a *Book of Records* and that provided us with plenty of material for the rest of the tour to mock each other with. I did some Skype calls in the evening.

We also learnt that one of the Munster players had been murdered and that created a lot of talk among the boys. It was massive news in Ireland, as you would expect, but it was pretty freaky stuff and unbelievable that he had been mistakenly killed. Replacement halfback Alby Mathewson arrived and caught up with us. The team for Saturday's test was announced to the public. I am getting a jersey engraved for Max. We get our own rooms at this stage of the week so that is always good. We also have the day off tomorrow, another cause for satisfaction. We were giving Neemiah Tialata a hard time tonight because Ted has asked him if he will give him a hair cut. Nay (Tialata) has become the team's unofficial team barber. It all started out when someone asked him to cut his hair and now he does anyone who asks. He even brings a set of clippers with him on tour. We were asking him what he might be talking about with Ted while he was cutting his hair.

Wednesday, 12 November

It was a day off training today. We had a media session for our usual pre-game interviews before the weekend. It was also a good day on the golf course as I won 50 euro off Ice. We had a pool session later and some of the guys went on a helicopter ride. It is great what some local people will offer you in the way of hospitality. I took the chance for the helicopter ride on an earlier tour and had a great look at Lansdowne Road from the air. Later on I caught up with some mates from Invercargill who were in Dublin for the game.

Thursday, 13 November

Things are starting to hot up now with the test in mind. At training our focus is attitude at the clean out, owning our own space, not getting taken out and our body height in rucks. It has to be said our backs training didn't go too well. Smithy wasn't happy. But we have to sharpen up because we will have a crowd of 83,000 people against us on Saturday, so how do we react? It was another poor training ground. We also shifted hotels to be closer to the venue and we now stay in a Hilton. Everyone was helping with moving the gear. There was an old man waiting at the hotel with a book that he wanted us all to sign. We get these sorts of requests all the time. I think he thought he might have been the only person asking for that sort of favour, but often we have 40–50 items that need to be signed at each city we go to. It can be a hassle getting everyone to sign every item, for various reasons.

We had a meeting with the Williments Travel tour party hosted by John McBeth and Keith Quinn tonight. They seemed most appreciative that we would make ourselves available for a night like this but we find it is great when we are so far away from home to walk into a room full of people speaking with Kiwi accents and talking about Kiwi things. It is a pleasant change, and it is also good as part of our build-up to the test. It gives you a real boost. We had our ticket allocation also today. We each get two tickets and there are generally about 20 extra tickets left over, so there are never enough for everyone's needs. What happens is that everyone who wants extra tickets writes their name and they are put into a hat and drawn out two at a time until they are all gone. So there are never any guarantees that you will be able to get the number of tickets you might want for a specific venue.

Friday, 14 November

Up for an early breakfast today. I thought a lot about Saturday's game during the night and am very excited about it. However, I also received the news that Hayley and Max were back in hospital again. It broke me this time; I couldn't help wondering whether I had made the right decision to come on the tour. Max had too much fluid around his lungs so they are changing his drugs to try to sort it out. We trained at Croke Park today and did the captain's run there. We don't usually train at the same venue as the captain's run, especially after we had England personnel filming one of our sessions on an earlier tour. It was quite funny going into the stadium in the bus, as the driver thought he could get under the maximum height barrier, but he ended up being too high and we had a few anxious moments sitting there when the roof scraped the barrier. There were plenty of comments made to the driver by the boys about that.

At the captain's run, I always wear my new boots to help wear them in. They are World Cuppers and I change them fairly regularly. I've got plenty of old boots at home, although I've also given plenty away over the years. I also wore my thermals during the session and think I will give them a run tomorrow. I sorted out where I will sit and staked my claim. This is something we do at every ground we play at, and we usually return and sit in the same spot when we return for future games, although I must admit I am unlikely to sit in the same place at Millennium Stadium when we play there. We were all made aware of the historical significance of Croke Park as a result of Snake's history lesson about the time the English Army came in and shot Irish people watching a Gaelic football game. That gave us an insight as to why the ground was so special and why it had been decreed that any game of British origin would never be played at the ground. It was massive that we should be given the chance to play at the ground. It is a great stadium. It is windy because the wind whistles through the area where the people were killed on what is known as Hill 16. It has never been built up in the way the rest of the ground has. The crowd is also further back from the playing field than usual but there is still a great atmosphere.

Afterwards I did some shopping in town for Max, to get a camera and to buy some toiletries. I did some stretches also as I usually do on the night before a game. I rang home as well. As part of our preparation we watched a DVD about Irish rugby in 2007. They pumped up hard for their games, that's for sure. It was different to how we approach games. There was plenty of passion flowing from the coach when he was talking to the side. We also did some more analysis of the Irish scrummaging.

Saturday, 15 November

Kick-off is at 5.15 pm. We have a walk through at 12 noon. I collected my jersey before 1.30 pm and folded it so the emblem was showing. I looked at the caps and the date. There was still an hour and 15 minutes before our 3.35 pm team meeting so I rang home and talked to Hayley.

I cleaned my boots next and put my boots in the bag first and then my jersey. I was feeling good after my phone call and thinking a lot about Hayley and Max as they are in Starship over the weekend. Hails is watching the game at Ronald McDonald House. The pre-game warm-up went well and we were able to take a 22–3 win from the game. It was a good feeling afterwards and you are always satisfied when you win. There was also a sense of relief but it capped what had been a happy big week preparing for the match. I played for Hails and Max. We had a formal after-match function to attend. I must admit I had two pints of Guinness; you can't go to Ireland without having one. The only time I have ever drunk Guinness is when I have been in Ireland. I rang Mum afterwards, as I do after every game. I was also told I will be on the bench for the Munster game. I had no trouble going to sleep.

Sunday, 16 November

Everyone helped pack our bags on the truck at 11.30 am and we were able to catch the train for Munster at 1 pm. Played some cards on the train and updated my diary. It was wet and cold when we arrived in Limerick. In the evening we went to a show about Munster against the All Blacks in 1978. It was a bit boring but it helped our motivation for Tuesday's game.

Monday, 17 November

We had a captain's run this morning for the team to play Munster while in the afternoon I had to train with the side that will play Wales at the weekend. We had to have an indoor session. I also did some 'stretcher-cise' in the evening as part of my pre-game ritual. Also ticked off my laundry to make sure it was all accounted for when it was returned.

Tuesday, 18 November

It might be game day but I have a contact training session at 9 am with the Wales team. It is back to the hotel for lunch and then a walk through with the side playing Munster at 2.30 pm. I have been to the university where we are training, and back to the hotel again, so many times over the past two days that it is not funny. It is actually quite a hard thing to get used to. Brad Thorn and I are the only ones involved and we commented to each other about how tiring it is. We don't usually play midweek games so it is something a bit different.

There was an awesome atmosphere before the game and Munster were fired up and really put some pressure on. It was a close game and I got on for the last 10 minutes. I managed to make the winning pass to Joe (Rokocoko) who scored to deny Munster its own chance for glory. Doug Howlett was playing for Munster so I caught up with him afterwards and had a couple of beers, which was a first for game week. But I am thinking I shouldn't be so anal about that. I bought Max a Munster jersey and had a walk through a packed town afterwards.

Wednesday, 19 November

We travelled to Cardiff on a charter flight. There is no doubt we are in rugby country. Customs are so easy when you arrive in Cardiff with the All Blacks. We went through a room to complete our procedures and were treated well. They even had a bus on the tarmac for us. We tend to be well-treated in most places, although Ireland is one place that is a bit more complicated. When we come back to New Zealand from a tour we are generally given specific instructions about which door to go through, which is different to what the public use. It is mainly because we have a whole lot of gear that would clog up the X-ray machines for ages.

We had some rubs in the morning as part of our recovery. The boys were very happy with the win over Munster and we couldn't help thinking about what might have happened had we lost. Would there be a play about us in 30 years' time? That seemed to be the question on most of the boys' minds. We unloaded our gear at the hotel. In the evening we had a fund-raising dinner for the New Zealand Rugby Foundation which does so much work for players affected by spinal injuries. Former Welsh star and British Lion John Taylor was the MC. Andy Leslie spoke about the work of the foundation and told us that one young New Zealander had died this year and two more would be unable to make a full recovery. It is a very sad side of the game.

We felt good about being able to help raise money for the cause. It was interesting how many overseas businessmen were prepared to pay for a table at the function where they would have the chance to have an All Black sit at their table. Hayley is sick back at home, which is a concern for me.

Thursday, 20 November

Because of our midweek game the test side was named later, although we had a fair idea earlier in the week because of our training sessions. I am starting at fullback. We had a media session again. I received a present and a card for Max from a member of the public.

Friday, 21 November

Captain's run again today at Millennium Stadium. I definitely chose a different seat from that I had last year at the World Cup, and so do most of the other guys who were there. I have also sorted out an engraved jersey for Max from tomorrow's game.

Saturday, 22 November

Another big game for us today and Cardiff was anticipating its chance for a win. The scene was set for a big stand-off after the haka as both teams stood their ground staring each other out. It was electric. However, the boys were unaffected and responded with a 29–9 win to keep our recent record intact and our hopes of a grand slam now centred on the England game.

Sunday, 23 November

Travelled down to London with the boys feeling excited about the win over Wales and ready to take our chance as it came.

Monday, 24 November

We trained at a flash school today, although the weather was freezing. Heard today that Max's operation date was confirmed for either 8 or 15 December. We had the last of our team activities for the tour. We had to do a skit and the winners will get double money for their efforts.

Tuesday, 25 November

I made the starting XV for the England game, my third game in succession. Training was held in very cold conditions. We attended the launch of the Pure New Zealand opening of the big rugby ball in London which is being used to promote the 2011 Rugby World Cup in New Zealand. The Queen attended and we met her. We had to wait for ages in the cold but the display was awesome. I have met the Queen a few times now and the last time she asked me how things were going and before I finished telling her she had moved on to the next person. Mind you, we also met our new Prime Minister, John Key, who was there, and he asked me if

I was keeping out of trouble. I was tempted to ask him, 'What have you heard?' It is always very special to meet the Queen, but to meet the Prime Minister as well was great. We had a gym session later and then our media session. In the evening we had a team dinner out. After that Ma'a Nonu and I visited the casino beside the team hotel. We had been there two years earlier when we toured, and they remembered us. They still had our details on file. But we only take £20 with us and generally just bet on our own numbers in roulette. We won £250, which isn't too bad when you translate it to New Zealand money. We did hope we hadn't used up all our luck before the last match.

Wednesday, 26 November

This was a big day for me in a total non-rugby sense. I went out on my own to visit a friend in the country, Nick Buckley. I had to get to where he was on the Underground and then catch the right train. Once I met him we then drove down to Leicester to meet with some more mates before I came back to the team hotel. I was away from 7 am to 8 pm on what I felt was a great expedition as I had to completely find my own way around. Normally on an All Blacks tour all you have to do is turn up at the right time and everything is done for you, so I was quite chuffed to do all that and get back in time for rubs in the evening. It was great to be able to get out of the hotel environment.

Thursday, 27 November

A full-on session of training today. We learnt about the Air New Zealand crash off Perpignan, which was sad news. We had a team lesson about Sir Edmund Hillary's achievements because the game at the weekend was the first time we would be playing for the Sir Edmund Hillary Shield, which will be used in future games with England. We learnt all about the great man and what he had done with his fame after conquering Mt Everest, especially his work in Nepal. His phrase after they climbed Everest, 'We knocked the bastard off', became our call as we prepared for the last game in the Grand Slam. It is always good to have something extra to play for and something in his memory was extra special. We had our team skits in the evening and then in the casino Ma'a had some more success.

Friday, 28 November

We had the captain's run in the morning and found Twickenham was cold. Ma'a and I had the grand final of our drop-kicking competition at Twickenham. We have this at every ground we play at. We kick from each side of the field and from various other places. We came into the final locked at 4–4 so it was sudden death and Ma'a was the winner. During the day Adidas announced that it had renewed its contract with the NZRU. I bought Max an England jersey and in our poker game in the evening Richie McCaw took the winnings.

Saturday, 29 November

Finally game day has arrived and while the game is important I am really looking forward to going home tomorrow. It was a great game. I was lucky enough to dot down twice in our 32–6 win. We won our Grand Slam, the third by an All Blacks team and my second. I have to say that the Slam meant more to me this time than earlier. The first one was by a team that had been together for a couple of years. But this team had gone through a lot with all the changes that were made after the World Cup. It was a totally different team and the success felt more special because of that. We didn't let a try in during the whole Grand Slam, and there were guys in the side who had not played a lot of international rugby so it was special from that viewpoint.

We had a couple of hours to fill in before the after-match so we had a few beers in the changing room. One of the bath tubs was full of beer so we sat in the baths singing 'Swing Low Sweet Chariot' and plenty of New Zealand songs while drinking. It is not something we really get to experience in New Zealand. After the game I gave Mick Byrne my jersey as my way of saying thanks for all the help he had given me. He will be missed, although we will still have the odd visit from him. We had a debrief in the changing room and sat down and reflected on our efforts as a team. Our after-match function was a black tie affair and once it was completed we felt as if the tour was finally over. It had been a great success and we enjoyed a celebration back at the hotel.

Graham Henry: 'Mils is a very balanced person'

I actually had a role in getting Mils to Auckland. I was headmaster of Kelston Boys' High School and the 1st XV coaches said they were keen to get him in the side for 1997. So I was involved to some extent in him coming to Auckland. However, I resigned at the end of 1996 so I didn't have a lot to do with him.

He is an outstanding footballer who has the ability to read situations whether playing at centre or fullback. He is outstanding in both positions. I do remember he started at centre in the 2003 Super 12 final against the Crusaders but at halftime we moved him back to fullback for the second half, and if we hadn't done that we wouldn't have won the game.

The problem we had as All Blacks selectors was that he was very good in both positions and in some circumstances he was a much better centre than we had available. After Tana retired we did not have a lot available at 13. While Conrad Smith and Richard Kahui have come through now, we did not have a lot of choice earlier. And with Leon MacDonald playing so well at fullback we were able to use Mils at centre.

At fullback he reads the game very well. His positional sense is excellent and he communicates well with his wings. He knows where the wings should be which reduces the pressure on him. He's very good under the high ball — the best in New Zealand. But that's because he practises it a lot. He has a great attacking awareness and, in more recent years, he has been able to stay on his feet longer than he used to. That means he can plough on ahead when the pass is not on and stay up until support arrives. He's the best fullback in the world at the moment.

He didn't play centre at all in 2008 and his last game there was in the World Cup, but he is a really suitable player for the position. He has a good catch and pass and his timing is pretty good. He gets into the right position defensively and he is very good defensively because he reads the attack so well.

We included him in the leadership group we set up in 2004 because he was a key player who was going to continually be picked for the All Blacks. His position in the team was never under question and to be a leader it is pretty important that you play regularly. He might give the impression of being shy but he has a lot of confidence in his own ability and he is respected by the other guys. With the Polynesian influence in the side, it is important to have balance there, and it is important to make sure the leadership is representative. Different people push different buttons and he has the ability to push buttons.

One of his major strengths is that he has the ability to push other people. Many are inclined to be reticent about being demanding of others but Mils, like Richie, is demanding of others. That is quite outstanding for the All Blacks because leading by example as they do puts pressure on others.

Mils is a very balanced person. He understands it is not all about you. He puts the team before himself, and his family before himself. It's a huge asset he has got. In challenging situations being an All Black has been a positive for him because he has learnt about resilience.

When his son was born before the 2008 Grand Slam tour, he was desperate to be there to assist the team, but he also knew he had to do the right things by his family. Hayley understands that and although Max had problems she knew he should go on the tour.

Like a lot of the group of players we have, there is a sense of unfinished business about their careers. They would like to win a World Cup. These are challenging times and as a group they are obviously trying to stick together. This team has a marvellous winning record and the only negative is the lack of a Rugby World Cup.

For Mils, his future is about staying as a whole. His body is asking him a few questions and he can't continue to play 10 months a year. He will look at how he continues to play, and he may have to take some time out of the game in order to continue. How he does that will be interesting. Because he doesn't want to let anyone down.

Captaincy and the future

Before the 2008 Super 14 season Ian Foster wanted us to go away and discuss who might be captain of the Chiefs. Jono Gibbes was passionate about doing it, which we were happy about, and then after the game against the Hurricanes, Gibbes got injured. It was a big week for me. I had just found out Hayley was pregnant and then the group decided I should become captain. I had another talk with the coaches, and with hooker Tom Willis' experience as well to call on, I felt happy about taking on the role. It also gave me an opportunity to work a lot harder off the field.

After the frustration of the World Cup, I was keen to devote more time to the Chiefs. As an All Black I had been in and out of the side, missing most of the previous season due to the reconditioning programme. I hadn't been able to contribute as much as I wanted off the field and I was keen to work harder on that. Taking on the captaincy was daunting. I thought the captain always did all the talking, had all the

215

ideas and ran the team. But the more I learnt, the more I realised that wasn't necessarily the case. The fact that I wasn't so close to the action at fullback had been a concern for Fossie but we decided that Tom would talk with the referees on smaller matters, and on more serious matters I would be called up to talk. It worked well.

I learnt how to challenge the coaches on certain things and I became a bit of a sounding board for the players. It also gave me an insight into the management point of view of running a team. Management is actually like a separate team. There were things that upset me in the way the team functioned and I would come home from training frustrated over some aspect, such as the way the week was structured and wondering why we did certain things. I looked at how we could get the best out of players. Appreciating that some guys respond to pressure and others fold on it, I felt we needed to address that in the side. Stephen Donald was a classic example. He is a player who is unorthodox, who likes to do things a certain way and he doesn't need to be pressured into some things. A lot of the way we did things as a team was centred around what the manager wanted without the manager actually being included in our discussions, so I wanted him brought into that.

I also had the feeling that the Chiefs as a whole were happy to get up for one big game a year and they lacked the belief to have consistency in their play, and in success. I was probably a little hard on the guys in trying to get that message through, and Fossie said to me at the end of the season that I came into the side a bit grumpy at times. But I felt we should always want to make the top four and I always had that belief. There is great talent in the side but we couldn't turn that into consistent success. I suppose that was a result of the youthfulness of the team. They hadn't been exposed, as I had, to the likes of Carlos Spencer, Eroni

Clarke and Michael Jones, who insisted on that sort of commitment. Our guys thought it was fine to arrive five minutes early to training and slip into their kit and run out. In Auckland we would be an hour early to practice.

What also frustrated me was that most of the team weren't aware of the players who had made the jersey what it was, great guys who had played for the Chiefs like Deon Muir and Scott McLeod. There was no sense of history of the side. It was nice to be able to get that in there. Fossie let me set up my own things. I chose my group of leaders and explained that they needed to be running the team and that I expected them to be doing the work. Barking at young players all the time was not the way to lead the side. The leaders had to be barking at other leaders because that spoke more to the younger players about what was expected of them.

I talked to Sitiveni Sivivatu and Sione Lauaki before the start of the 2009 season about them being a lot more responsible about the way they acted. I have a good relationship with both of them and they want more responsibility. So they had to set an example and that involved being punctual and setting the scene for others. As a captain I like to see players getting out and talking to sponsors and I like to see greater harmony between upstairs and the players. If we buy into the way they are doing things, and what they are trying to achieve, we will have a greater understanding of what they want and things will work better. I've always said if the team plays well the financial things will take care of themselves. Finally, as a captain, I have got to perform on the field. My biggest worry is that if I don't perform my words won't mean anything. I can't do it all by myself and my co-leaders have got to help me run the team.

Coming back into the All Blacks at the start of 2008 was quite different to usual, after the disaster at Cardiff. The captaincy of the Chiefs gave me something to focus on and made it easier to concentrate. Another factor was having Faifili Levave stay with us in Hamilton in 2008 while he was part of the Chiefs franchise. He gave me an insight into how to get excited and motivated about rugby again. He made me realise I'm not that old and he took me back to those exuberant days of my early years. Faifili has a massive future if he sticks at the game. He plays in a similar style to Sione Lauaki, but if he stays fit and focused, and he is such a focused Island boy, he can go far. He also helped me with the food I was eating and helped me regain my desire by his infectious enthusiasm for rugby.

By the time the All Blacks side was picked to play the first test of 2008 against Ireland, we had lost quite a few players who had gone overseas. So there was a degree of nervousness, not only because it was our first game since the Cup, but because we held Ireland in high regard. They had never beaten us, but no one wanted to be in the team that lost for the first time. There was a sense, as we assembled, of wanting to undo some of the wrongs from the World Cup. Yet there was also a sense of excitement about playing again and proving that we still had pride in the All Blacks jersey. It was a different feeling to when I returned after the 2003 World Cup. Back in 2004 I wanted to keep my stake in the All Blacks and I was still young enough to be able to look ahead to 2007 which was the next chance. But this time there is some unease about 2011. Still now I am uncertain how long I will play and whether I will still have that excitement. I was devastated by the Cardiff result and four years is, all of a sudden, a bloody long time. I almost felt it might be too long. But 2008 was a little bit more special because of that. I realised that time was no longer on my side, it was limited and I should make the most of my tenure in the team.

After Cardiff, Gilbert Enoka put me onto Kerry Spackman and I worked with him on some of my off-the-field activities. He helped my motivation greatly; it was one of the best things I did. He got my mental game right, and to concentrate on what excited me about my life. I got into my diving and working on some university papers, and also heightened my excitement about the everyday activities I was doing for my rugby, even my drills that I needed to do. Kerry had me develop what he called the Winner's Bible. I would write down the things that made me happy each day and often I would reflect on those things before a test match. It was amazing to feel the heightened sense of excitement that gave me about the game. The important thing was the exciting things were not rugby specific.

Of course, our first game in 2008 was that game at Westpac Stadium in Wellington against Ireland. They were the worst conditions I have ever played in. I never experienced conditions like that even when I played in Invercargill. I went into the Irish dressing room afterwards, and usually after a side has been beaten it is fairly quiet but there was a heck of a lot of noise and movement as guys were trying to get warm.

We then played England in two tests, in Auckland and Christchurch. Once again they sent out a below-strength team but still managed to talk the team up as being competitive. I was a bit concerned before the Auckland test as I had trained under an injury cloud all week, but I was thankful to be able to play. There was a buzz around the team and our win started something of a belief that we could do again what we had done when rebuilding after 2003. We had new guys playing in Auckland but they settled in well to win their first test caps. Then we carried on to

Christchurch and did it again in what was another step up. Considering all the changes, we did an exceptional job and we were really satisfied that two of the three wins in those games had been pretty convincing. But England still managed to go away thinking they had done us in the forwards and it had only been our backs who beat them. It amuses us to hear that they left thinking they had the better of us. But for all the success we had we knew the Tri Nations would be the real tester. We knew the big one was always around the corner.

After that early loss to Australia, and our recovery a week later, we headed to Dunedin where we were defending our unbeaten record against South Africa on Carisbrook. We were conscious of that and were totally focused. It was a difficult game. We won a lot of ball but we couldn't convert it into points. We took our foot off the pedal and Ricky Januarie scored a good try to give them the game. I felt it was one of my better games, but I couldn't enjoy that feeling because it hurt so much to have shattered our record of never losing to South Africa at Carisbrook. However, we didn't have our sense of belief knocked out of us. We had always known it was going to be tough and close. But there were a lot of good things in what we did, although we didn't finish off our opportunities and we didn't put a lot of pressure on them.

We then headed to South Africa and managed to win there and keep South Africa scoreless. It was yet another example of how we could quickly turn things around, as we had against Australia. It is pretty difficult to go over there and keep them from scoring. But we had pride in our defence and we enjoyed keeping teams scoreless by asserting it. I have to admit the attraction in going to South Africa diminishes with each year. It is a long, long way to travel and while going there for Super 14 games is more relaxed because you have two or three games there, and you can get yourself into it more, the test match trips are tougher. The whole country gets wound up and there is an excitement you can feel. But it is hard when you can't even walk down the street in some of the cities for safety reasons. You are basically confined to your room, and that can be frustrating. And game parks don't get too exciting after you have been to see them so many times. Finding something different to do seems to be the hardest thing over there.

An extra factor in 2008 was the introduction of the Experimental Law Variations (ELVs) which became almost the wholesale responsibility of southern hemisphere sides. At the Chiefs we looked to try to nail the advantages that we could from the changes. One that we especially worked on was if we were tackled we had to throw the ball back quickly. We practised it a lot and Fossie nailed it hard. There was a lot more kicking, more to keep the ball in, while we had to remember not to carry the ball back into the 22-metre area before kicking.

At fullback it became a different type of game. You had to be fitter and cover more ground while you were required to do more kicking. With free kicks being awarded rather than penalties, you had to work out when and when not to go with a quick kick. There was so much hype leading up to the start of the season about the game being faster, guys had preconceived ideas about what to expect. From a captaincy point of view the challenge was to forget the old laws and think about how the team could adapt to the new variations. That was tricky because there was nothing to base judgements on. Rucks are always a talking point and referees seem to have different views, even among themselves, on the topic. One anomaly I feel needs to be addressed is when a defensive team getting tackled with the ball pushes back attackers. Too often the advantage in that situation goes to the attacking side. Why shouldn't the defensive team get the reward from dominating the tackle in that situation?

There is no doubt in my mind, though, that the rugby looks a lot better. It is more appealing and there are not so many penalties. The ELVs have freshened the game up a bit and made it tidier. The breakdown is always going to be a talking point. One of the reasons I think there has been so much opposition to the ELVs in the northern hemisphere is because of their driving type of game, especially from lineouts, where, under the old laws, you were not allowed to sack mauls. That was also a strong point of the South Africans. But I think the South Africans have adapted really well. The flair is also starting to come back into the game. The inside backs are able to have more time to control play due to the five-metre gap and they are able to find space. The positional requirements have changed a little. Ma'a Nonu is a classic example. He has started to use a lot more of his skills because the incentive, and space, is there to try to do more. Teams and players are a lot faster and fitter than they used to be, the forwards especially. They are now required to act like backs in open field play.

The fact that we had been exposed to the ELVs gave us a slight advantage when we played our home test matches in 2008. Although we had to revert to the old laws for those games we were a lot more explosive and a lot fitter and we aimed to spread the ball wider while also trying to win rucks faster. Then even more changes were required for the Tri Nations, which was played without quite so many of the ELVs being used. While it was difficult for us as players to adjust, the coaching panel had no experience of playing under the ELVs and they spoke to us about how we as a team could play the game under those circumstances. I think the unfamiliarity of having to coach under the ELVs was seen in some of the experimenting we did in the first game against the Aussies in Sydney. The coaches showed their ability to adapt quickly. Then, on the end-of-year northern hemisphere tour, we went back to penalties instead of free kicks and that tested our discipline.

They still seem to oppose the ELVs up north with their bash, bash, bash style of game. I think if we could find some way to take the Super 14 to Britain and show them how we played, I could guarantee the fans over there would enjoy it. The Super 14 is a whole lot better than European rugby. It is fast and dynamic, which is what spectators want to see. I'm sure they don't want to see 10-man rugby all the time.

The Super 14 itself is a great tournament. I would be happy to see it start a bit later and to have a play-offs system involving six or eight teams at the end. It is frustrating with a team like the Chiefs who are starting to get things together in the latter part of the season but being too late to take a play-offs place. At the moment it is more of a sprint where you have to win every week to make the semis. Some of the changes being talked about by the administrators are interesting and should only strengthen the competition. I would like to see it start later but go a bit longer. Everyone talks about it starting too soon with a lack of big crowds when people are still interested in cricket.

I believe there is an opportunity to make some massive inroads in overseas markets with rugby. It would be great to go to different places to give rugby exposure. It is something we have talked about as players. Something like having a franchise based in the United States would make the travel requirement a whole lot better and it would be quite good to go somewhere other than Australia or South Africa. And with some of their amazing NFL players over there, or players who miss out on making the grade, you would be able to build something to get it started.

As professionalism has developed in our rugby there have been huge changes since I first started. Now most players are represented by managers and there is a Players' Association which is looking out for players' lives after rugby, because it really is only a short time you have in the game, and you need to look after the dollars you have earned. The support side of rugby, through coaching structures and management of players both inside and outside of teams, has become a business, an industry of its own. I am quite certain that despite all the changes, and all the doomsayers who wonder about rugby's future, the game is in good shape and will continue to play a big part in New Zealand's social structure. Plenty of other players will have their chance to aspire to the game's highest levels and to live their own dream.